# *Woman Time*

# WOMAN TIME

*Personal Time Management for Women Only*

## DIANA SILCOX

### WITH MARY ELLEN MOORE

*Wyden Books*

*Manufactured in the United States of America.*
FIRST EDITION

Library of Congress Cataloging in Publication Data
Silcox, Diana.
    Woman time.

    Bibliography: p.
       1. Women—United States—Time management.
2. Housewives—United States—Time management.
3. Women—Employment—United States. I. Moore,
Mary Ellen, joint author. II. Title.
HQ1221.S58     640'.43'024042     80-5191
ISBN 0-87223-608-0

*Designed by Vincent Torre*

*To Larry—*

for his confidence, encouragement,
and love

# Contents

You Can Get Control   3

The Superwoman Myth   11

You're Not Guilty!   19

Go Ahead: Say No!   28

How to Put a Price On Your Time   33

The Blessings of Networking   47

Planning: Using the Master Key   54

Your Time Log Tells All   60

   *Daily Time Sheet*   66

Beware These Time-Robbers   69

A Word About a Dirty Word: "Procrastination"   72

Beating the Perfectionism Trap   79

Beating the Waiting-Time Bugaboo   84

Speak Up to Save Time   91

Delegation Protocol   101

Making Delegation Work at Work   112

Making Delegation Work at Home   117

Overcoming Telephone Hang-ups   126

How to Tame Drop-in Visitors   134

## Contents

Oh No, Not Another Meeting!    142

Crisis! The Nimble Art of Firefighting    146

How to Unclutter Your Life    148

What to Do When You've Too Much to Do    151

Keep a "To-Do" List    155

    *Daily "To-Do" List*    165

How to Establish Priorities    167

Flexibility: The Liberating Art of Loosening Up    175

Tips for Time-Conscious Women Travelers    181

Here's Time Just for You    191

How to Find Your Quality-of-Life Values    200

    *Quality-of-Life Goals*    208

Setting Your Career Goals    211

    *Goals: Two Months to Five Years from Now*    214

Coping with Morning Madness    221

    *Is Time on Your Side in the Morning?*    230

Home Tips    233

    *Shopping List*    242

TV or Not TV?    246

Home, Sweet Office    249

Time-Saving Tips for the Office    256

Husbands Are People, Too    265

Making Time for Sex    273

The Children's Hour    282

Time Off for Vacations    296

Alone at Last    301

Recommended Reading    307

# *Woman Time*

# *You Can Get Control*

---

I just want the merry-go-round to stop, so I can quit being dizzy.

—**KAREN OLSON**
*Insurance agent*

There is always time to do the things you really want to do.

—**ANONYMOUS**

WE ALL WANT MORE TIME, whether it's for working or playing, dreaming or doing, family or friends, or time just for ourselves.

We moan because there are only 24 hours in a day, yet we know it's an irrevocable fact. We cannot literally add hours to the day, but through good time management practice we can gain the edge on time.

I've always thought that I don't have much time to manage, that it's already managed for me. There are so many things that I have to do that it doesn't seem like I have many hours left.

—**ROSALIE DAVIES**
*Librarian and musician*

This woman sums up the universal feeling that time controls us, that there's no way we can control time. Not so! Time management is no elusive goal. When you apply its specifics to every

3

slice of your life—home, business, personal—you'll find time you thought you never had.

*Time is life.*

Alan Lakein, known as the father of time management, said it, and we all know how true the statement is. Time is your ultimate asset. When we waste our time, we're wasting our life, too precious a commodity to see gone with the wind or to remain dominated by males. And many men are only beginning to accept that women weren't born to spend their time running errands.

## FLEXIBILITY FOR YOU

If time management makes life wonderful, why aren't more people doing it?

> When I hear people talking about time management, it sounds very hard and regimented—like you should be spending every minute of your day making lists and doing meaningful things.
>
> —GENEVIEVE MEEK
> *Freelance illustrator*

Since women fill more roles than men, they have more time management problems. Yet many, including the woman above, fear the term itself. Time management sounds like just another "hard" thing to do; it creates new anxieties: Am I managing my time *perfectly?* Am I making the best use of *every minute of every day?*

Forget it! Time management in fact gives you flexibility—the choices that every life deserves, including the precious freedom to do spontaneous things, to have fun without losing control, without seeing the rest of your life crumble around you.

If the term "time management" sounds a little too formal, too intimidating, think of it as "controlling your time." And control is what you want, right?

*You needn't become a slave to time. We'll help you make time your servant.*

Another reason more people don't apply time management to their lives applies specifically to women: Until now, such principles have been applied only to the office.

But you need hardly be reminded that women do not function in a vacuum. We're also mothers, wives, lovers, housekeepers, chauffeurs, friends—and we don't have the life-support system that was always available to our male counterparts—a wife at home to ease all his other roles. We need help, lots of it!

Now working women are a major fact of life. Yet we're still not free to devote full attention to our careers. The responsibility for maintaining our homes—husbands' and children's wants and needs, housekeeping duties, endless errands—is still our responsibility.

Most men may "help us out" occasionally, but helping out is a small drop in our bucket of responsibilities. Until we evolve a life-style with our men *sharing equally* the responsibilities (other than career), women face completely different time problems: Lack of time doesn't simply frustrate us; it absolutely overwhelms us! Very few women seem able to find a Sunday afternoon free to watch football on television, a pursuit our men have always found time for.

I first became involved in time management when I started my own office systems business and realized I was working all the time. My social life had deteriorated until it reached the point where I didn't know what sensible people did on a weekend anymore. I had vague memories of the theater, the ballet, and reading for enjoyment, not just for work. I realized I was becoming very one-dimensional and, in desperation, turned to time management as espoused by Lakein.

5

I began to apply the basic philosophies underlying time management to my business life. I—

- Focused on accomplishing only what *absolutely* must be done in order to provide extra "discretionary time"—time when you're free to do what *you* choose
- Made the right choices (it's far more important to use your time *effectively* by accomplishing one or two jobs, than to be *efficient* and undertake but not complete many jobs)
- Broke my old time mold and established new patterns based on my priority goals and objectives (Priorities are the most important of all your life values, goals or to-do activities— without priorities you're lost)
- Became flexible; when I planned my time, I allowed for the unexpected or a shift in my priorities

It worked so well that I began to advise my clients on time management, started workshops and seminars, and began speaking at business organizations' functions.

Ultimately I was asked by the Gillette Company to do a study of women's habits for its personal care division.

This study of 300 women (working, nonworking, mothers, single, married with no children) was the first to look at the time problems of women. Not surprisingly, we found them to be much different from those of men because of women's multiroles, unsupported by a wife at home.

The study turned up something else: Almost all the women in the study, the women I met on the subsequent promotional tour and the women I counseled, made the almost desperate plea:

"Where do I find *time for me?*"

## NEW: TIME MANAGEMENT AT HOME

Time management had never been applied to the home and personal fronts. I realized that I had subconsciously taken the basic principles and applied them to my own personal life, which was why time management had worked such wonders for me. When I had set my lifetime goals, they were not all business directed. There were things I wanted for my personal achievement, and the only way to do that was to completely separate my personal life from my business life—which is what I did.

I admit—it was a scary move. I thought, *Oh my God, how am I going to accomplish this? The book says . . . If I only do the important things, that's all that's important in life.* Despite my fear that my business would go down the drain, I was determined to try it.

I set a minimum of six to eight months to see if there was any improvement. The result is I have more time available to me than ever—the theater is once again a reality, not just a pleasant memory.

Essentially, time management is the same no matter where you practice it: office, home, personal life. Working women have more demands on their time than anybody else, so—if they really want to gain more discretionary "time for me"—they should start putting the principles into practice.

And it's not easy. There's no one magical answer that's going to give you more time tomorrow, after you finish reading this book, than you have today. But neither is it impossible:

I've done it; women I've worked with have done it; and women I know who apply time management to their lives can attest to the results.

Think of time management like a diet. You know you're not

going to lose weight just by reading one of the numerous books on the market. You're going to check out the diets and choose the one that's right for you. Then you're going to begin the difficult task of cutting down (or supplementing or whatever) your food intake. If you're as human as the rest of us, you'll probably backslide a little. As you continue the diet, it'll become easier and easier until you've finally reached your ideal weight. But even then you must stick to a maintenance plan or all your intense dieting will have been in vain.

## NO EFFICIENCY EXPERTS NEEDED

The end result, as any successful dieter knows, is well worth the trouble.

So it is with time management. Choose the principles that apply to your own life-style; apply them; if you backslide, don't dismiss the idea of time planning; just get back on the track. You'll notice in a surprisingly short time that it's becoming a natural part of your life, particularly because the results of good time management begin to show up *immediately*. And once you see these results, there should be no problem with maintenance.

I don't intend to turn you all into little efficiency machines: up at six—make the bed—five steps to the bathroom—oops, should have woken Janey first . . .

You should do *less* and do it more effectively; not do *more* and do it efficiently. That is, you can work effectively toward your goals, not worry about all the other things that surround you.

Women are already doing far too much without having to worry about doing everything to perfection. So time management for women encourages you to do less by setting realistic goals and clear priorities so you'll see beyond the details that so often trap us, bore us, and bog us down.

We're not going to tell you how to become Superwoman; we're going to show you why it's unnecessary to become Superwoman!

## TO EACH HER OWN TIME

Just as one diet is not correct for everyone, there is no one *right* way to gain control of your time. Everybody's priorities are different, depending on family size and needs, personal likes and dislikes. One woman may get up an hour earlier than absolutely necessary so she can clean her house or study for a speech or weave a tapestry; another would rather sleep to the last possible minute and clean her house or shop at 2:00 a.m.!

It's important to recognize these differences, to know your own peak hours and your own priorities and then to tailor your time to fit them. That's you controlling time, not time controlling you. The key to this goal is the same for everybody: planning. And your own planning should consider these aspects of your life—

*Your quality-of-life values:* We can't really begin to make plans until we know what we want out of life. Good family relationships? Wealth? A high-powered career? We've nevertheless put the section on setting quality-of-life values toward the end of the book; that'll give you a chance to see your choices when you consider your own values, and what steps to take to achieve these values.

*Your goal-setting:* Once we know what our values are, we can begin setting definite, attainable goals.

*Your priorities:* Priority comes up a lot in time management. We establish priorities for our values, for the goals leading to the values, even for the daily activities which lead us to the goals. Without a clear set of priorities, time management is a muddy image, not an achievable way of life. We talk about your highest priorities (the A-1's) and lowest priorities (the C-4's, which, by the way, can usually be done away with), and all the in-between priorities (A-3's, B-2's, and so forth).

*Your activities:* These are the doable things that make time management much less overwhelming and intimidating. An activity accomplished today can lead to a goal accomplished next week.

Just as planning is the key to time management, so is realism the key to its success. When we diet, we cannot realistically say "I'm going to lose ten pounds today or else" and do it. To control time, we cannot say "I'm going to be president of my bank tomorrow" and do it. It's a gradual process, and we're going to be realistic about your time.

Time management is different for women for another major reason: Women's time conflicts (home vs. office, children vs. husbands, everything else vs. us) produce less-than-tangible time-wasters: Guilt about not being the Superwomen we think we should be makes it much more difficult to gain control of our time because we're trying to do everything and be everything to everyone. Since time management tries to eliminate such time-wasters as guilt, women must come to grips with the Superwoman myth and its debilitating effects before tackling the basics of time management.

Coping with your inner conflicts makes coping with your other conflicts much easier. Then it's on to the ticks and tocks of time management which will yield time you thought you never had—time, as it should be, for *you.* We promise!

# The Superwoman Myth

One thing I learned early when Jimmy was governor is that you can't dress and have your hair and your fingernails perfect all the time. When Jimmy was elected governor, Amy was about three years old, and I tried to keep her perfect too. You can't do it. Jimmy used to drill that into me. In Plains, we didn't have a restaurant, so Jimmy would bring everybody home for lunch from the warehouse, and I would fix them sandwiches. The house might not be spotless, but he would sit me down and say, "You did the best you could—that's all you can do." You learn that if you're going to do the things you want to do, you can't be perfect, and once you accept that you can relax.

—ROSALYNN CARTER
People *interview*

Never envy the other person; you just can't see the other half which would equal things.

—DR. O. A. BATTISTA

THE SUPERWOMAN MYTH has so successfully distorted our own perceptions of who we should be and what women can do that most of us feel frustrated and angry because we're not leaping buildings with a single bound.

The very term "Superwoman" implies that anyone who isn't super is something less, an implication few egos can accept without asking, "Where am I failing?" But *are* we failing?

Whenever we compare ourselves with others—women we know well, women we're merely acquainted with or even women we've just heard or read of—we can *always* find something that we're not doing that these other women are. If you insist on making comparisons, you might follow up the initial look at what they're doing with a thorough check of your own doings. Busy as most of us are, the score evens up remarkably quickly.

An even better solution is to stop making comparisons entirely. Wondering whether we'll be as successful as our next-door neighbor will only trip us up. We need to remove the stumbling blocks before us now—not add a few more.

## WHERE SUPERWOMAN COMES FROM

It's only natural to try to be the best at whatever we're doing, which for women today includes being the best on the job, the best mother, the best wife, the best housekeeper. Unfortunately, the *best* is usually an image waved at us by people who do not have to be the best in *all* these roles, so they can afford to be extravagant in the portrayal of women.

The television commercial that best reflects how others see us, implying that this is how we should see ourselves, is the perfume commercial featuring a model who quick-changes from housewife-mother-cook to professional person to sexy wife, all to the lyrics of "I'm a Woman." "The eight-hour perfume for your 24-hour woman," the commercial extols.

The fact that a marketing executive somewhere recognizes that today's women are *24-hour* women is, perhaps, indicative of our progress. Still, it's a fact: we can't do it all by ourselves perfectly. Even attempting such a feat would take a drastic toll on our mental and physical health.

So why do we try?

We attempt to live up to the Superwoman myth for some very convincing reasons:

1. Media image.
2. Keeping up with Ms. Jones.
3. Tradition.

The Superwoman syndrome is the root of our time problem. "On the psychological level," says Dr. Sarah Slagle, a clinical psychologist and psychotherapist in private practice in New York City and Scarsdale, and also a wife and mother of two, "it's been suggested that some women are still not comfortable with assertive or aggressive aspects of being career women; they have to prove their femininity by being *super* wives and mothers as well. I think this is changing rapidly. It's becoming much more acceptable for a woman to be assertive and still feel feminine. Still, the pattern a woman learned at home of what's expected of a woman by what she saw her mother and father do can be very ingrained. A woman can still feel guilty if she doesn't fill the roles she saw her mother fill as bed maker and cookie baker.

"Husbands, too have expectations based on what they experienced in their own homes," continues Dr. Slagle. "There's research to show that a man whose mother worked is much more encouraging of his wife working and is willing to be more flexible in sharing the homemaking tasks. I grew up in a home where my father did a major share of the cooking. My husband enjoys cooking, which I don't particularly, so in our home, too, he does most of the cooking.

"I recall being a little taken aback when I read a questionnaire my seven-year-old son filled out in school for Mother's Day. In answer to the question 'My mother's favorite food is _____,' he wrote, 'my father's waffles,' and in answer to 'The dish my mother cooks best is _____,' he wrote, 'my mother doesn't cook.'

When I thought about this more, I felt, 'That's all right—he'll be quite liberated.' Now when his father is traveling, my son makes the waffles.

"I think it's important for women to see that *these role expectations weren't written down in heaven* and that they're really quite alterable. Trying to be Superwoman leads to a lot of stress and dissatisfaction."

Living up to the myth requires every time-waster known, especially perfectionism and overcommitment. And yet the myth is perpetuated by many well-meaning people who tell us in books and seminars and magazines how we can be more *efficient:* how we can accomplish everything with no sweat, how we can be sexier, how we can be better mothers, wives, workers, lovers— how we can be all things to all people, except probably to ourselves.

The solution is not learning how to do it *all more efficiently,* but learning how to do *less more effectively,* which is what time management is all about:

WORK (AND PLAY) SMARTER, NOT HARDER.

## YOU'RE NOT INEXHAUSTIBLE

The media picture of women as something other than mortal runs deeper than the simplistic and sometimes insulting TV commercials. No matter how many good intentions lie behind the bombardment of the public with images of the crème de la crème of womanhood, we end up wondering, "Why can't I be like her?" or "What's wrong with me?"—"instead of," points out Dr. Doris Moss, former director of New York's Interpersonal

Counseling Center and currently executive director of Abused Women's Aid in Crisis, "What's wrong with her?"

There's nothing "wrong" with either woman. We just don't see the sacrifices, compromises and tensions that make so-called Superwomen mere mortals like the rest of us. "It's OK to be tired and frazzled at the end of the day," says Dr. Moss. "The only time it isn't OK is if you've internalized this kind of image and you're feeling rotten about yourself."

Unfortunately, no matter how aware we are of the fallacy of media portrayal, we will still let it influence us.

Linda Koe, mother of two, wife, and a commercial banking representative in Independence, Missouri, says with a touch of humorous despair: "I feel like I should be striving to be . . . Wonder Woman. I have bought the cultural and media image—*I* can do all *that*. And of course, I *don't* still do all that."

Judy Sommerschield of Chicago, another mother of two, wife and owner of Schield Personnel, also laughs wryly when she admits to making desserts from scratch even though "I don't mind it, but I do not love it. I'm sure I do it because I feel that one of the roles of a woman is to produce homemade cookies. The commercials have convinced me."

Since we have trouble disengaging ourselves from the media's image, it's even more difficult for our children to distinguish between reality and fantasy. Manhattan insurance agent Karen Olson's daughter Robin attended a day nursery school which required that the parents of the students must be working.

"I sometimes have to play shrink," Olson, a single parent, explains, recalling that "when Robin was in kindergarten, one night she asked me, 'Why can't you stay home with me like other mommies do?' She was in school from eight to six. So I asked her, 'What mommies do you know that do that?' She had a terrible time thinking of any such mommies and finally she said, 'Mrs. Brady on TV.'"

As a result of this popular image of the woman as inexhaustible and expert in all her roles, many of us, subconsciously or consciously, try to emulate the *visible* parts of the image.

At one point in her life, Margo Berk-Levine, owner of Temporarily Yours and Margo Berk Personnel (two Manhattan agencies), wife and mother of two sons, found herself "very resentful, very depressed and not looking within, but looking at externals. My first reaction had been 'I can't handle two children and a husband and a job like thousands of other people do, because there's something wrong with me, obviously some inadequacy.' "

Keeping up with Ms. Jones is nothing new. Keeping up with the Joneses is a classic trait of Americans; we've always striven to have two cars just like the neighbors, not realizing that the neighbors owe the bank their first-born female child.

The comparisons are killing us. Just as you cannot compare apples to oranges, neither can you compare two women with different priorities, different life values, different biorhythms.

Unfortunately, it's very easy to fall into this trap. The only way to avoid it is to occasionally take time out and objectively run a check on your own motives for doing what you're doing. It requires brutal honesty with yourself.

Are you doing this or that because you really *want* to be doing it? Because it'll lead to your ultimate goal? Because you enjoy doing it?

Or are you doing it because your next-door neighbor seems to be doing it? Or because you think others expect it of you?

Unless you begin to run this objective self-evaluation you're going to find your wheels spinning in too many wrong directions to enable you to get control of your time. Keeping up with Ms. Jones is a great way for time to gain control over you.

The media are not entirely to blame. There's that old bugaboo that never lets us forget what our own mothers and grandmothers did: tradition.

Tradition is fine, up to a point, that point being today. Mom and grandma may have had the whitest laundry in town, but probably they didn't also go to an office every day. But even when the traditional role models don't apply to us personally, we're still too conscious of them.

Since women have traditionally been responsible for both the upkeep of the house and the well-being of its occupants, we figure if our mothers could do it, we should be able to do it too. Even though, for the most part, our mothers didn't work.

As Susan Edmiston wrote in *Savvy*, the working woman "was heroically trying to merge her new feminine aspirations with old traditional values. 'Women who choose careers react to the cultural expectations of femininity by trying to prove themselves in all spheres,' Columbia sociologist Cynthia Epstein wrote in 1970. 'They accept all the role expectations attached to their female status, feeling that to lack any is to deny that they are feminine.' In short, working women were determined to outcook, outlook, and out-mother stay-at-home wives. To fail in any part of the feminine role would be to fail as a woman."

## HOW BARBARA MANAGES

Barbara Kulicke started a picture-framing business with her husband in the 1950s. It has grown into an extremely successful company, Kulicke Frames in New York. As a role model she had her own mother, who helped her father with his business and at the same time raised Barbara. In turn, Barbara, who took brief time out to have two children of her own, relied on housekeepers to help her raise the children while she worked. She viewed the multiple roles as natural:

"It was just a reflex," she says now. "I didn't even think about it. I know that my role was to help my husband get his business moving, and that's what I did—that and everything else. It's a triple-shifting Superwoman kind of thing, to have a huge load to carry and do it very well."

Now, at 50, Kulicke has bought out the business from her husband and sold it to a large corporation, although she remains president of the Kulicke Frames division. Her children are grown. Her daughter is now a mother herself and helping her own husband with a business. Kulicke is also divorced. The detachment from the busy life that was simply reflex has given her time to think about that life, rather than just react:

"I didn't know I was a Superwoman. I didn't know I was a slave until somebody told me. It's essential that you see it. And then it can be altered. I think the woman has to say, 'That's it. I'm not going to do it all anymore unless things change.'"

Sometimes it's difficult to see how you can get out of that trapped feeling of having to be Superwoman simply to survive. This is where learning to manage time effectively aids us; it helps us to establish the priorities that will make us spot anything that's not necessary. With priorities clearly established, we're able to ignore the superfluous and finally get control of time and pull our lives together.

Once you recognize and accept the fact that being Superwoman isn't so great (or realistic), you're halfway to the point of taking charge of your own life.

# You're Not Guilty!

*At a certain point, I realized . . . there are things you can give up without giving up being "a good mother."*
— MARGO BERK-LEVINE
*Employment agency owner*

ONE OF THE MOST prevalent (and destructive) feelings that women experience is guilt.

Working mothers feel guilty because they must leave their children with outside child care.

Working wives feel guilty because they're unable to cook dinner every night or keep the house as clean as their husbands are accustomed to.

Working single women feel guilty for a Catch-22 reason: If they're successful in their career, they feel guilty because they haven't lived up to their mother's expectations vis-à-vis husband, home, and children. If they're not successful, they feel guilty because they think they haven't worked hard enough.

All working women feel guilty because they insist, *"I'm not doing enough."* Especially if—God forbid!—a woman finds a few extra minutes for herself.

Guilt is an impetus to do more, do it faster, do it better, do it with quantitative *and* qualitative value. Unfortunately, it's an unhealthy, emotionally costly impetus, and by *reacting* to the negative feelings of guilt, we too frequently overlook the positives of what we're doing or should be doing.

That's the bad news.

The good news is that as women discover it's OK to share their feelings, guilt has come out of the closet. By now, numerous studies prove that our reasons for feeling guilty, whatever they are, are invalid.

Even better news is that women are coming to grips with their guilt by making positive efforts to put it in perspective.

Since we're managers of our time as well as our feelings, feeling guilty is all but an abdication of our own management capabilities. Rather than feel sorry for ourselves, and guilty that we're not doing something, which is debilitating, we should ask ourselves what we can be doing to make us feel better about ourselves.

You can't do this without very clear priorities (there's that word again!); and for many women, this requires discussing priorities with the family. When you accept the entire burden of your career and your household, you're asking for trouble as long as others are involved in your life.

Suppose you do set priorities and manage your time accordingly, and then something doesn't work. Well, you still know you've done your best. But when you don't make positive choices, the negatives almost always take over. We become martyrs and doormats. Unless we choose to snap out of it, guilt becomes something of a luxury—though still hardly desirable.

## HOW TRADE-OFFS WORK

Women are beginning to realize that guilt is not a very attractive or productive feeling. Dr. Doris Moss says: "I think those pressures (of conflicting roles) go on, but I think women are coming to grips with their feelings of guilt about trade-offs.

Are they sacrificing one person to make the other happy? Are they sacrificing their obligations or their feelings of obligations at home in order to handle their careers?

"One of the ways to come to grips with it is just to come to grips with it. Say: 'This is something I have to look at, think about and not just muddle along and hope everything's going to be all right.' I think women have to accept the fact that there are some trade-offs, and try to handle them and try to minimize what they consider their negative effects."

Margo Berk-Levine began making such trade-offs by trial and error. She "gave up" cooking a full meal for her family every night. She was running her two personnel services, putting in long hours. "I began to ask my housekeeper to do little things like setting the table, making the salads. She could bathe one of the children. You begin to work things out; little things to begin with—but it's all a help."

Seeing what a help it was and realizing that her family was not suffering permitted Berk-Levine to "come to grips" with initial feelings of guilt. Obviously, such guilt is often wrapped up in conflicting roles. We slight one role to give attention to the other.

The reason? The puritan work ethic, and it's been drummed into us since childhood. Even girl children, although they may not be taught the *career* work ethic, learn from early on that we're lazy if we're not always doing something visibly productive.

Susan Schein, owner of Double Ess Unlimited, a Manhattan promotion and public relations firm, is a single woman who believes in being good to herself, yet feels twinges when she is good to herself:

"I must say that I feel too guilty. I grew up in a household that practiced puritan ethics. My father believed you work 17 hours a day if it takes 17 hours to get the job done. And you toe the line and you are a perfectionist. Therefore, if I set out to do five things in a day and it takes me only two hours to do those five things, I'll feel guilty, instead of saying 'Great! You can accomplish that much!' Some days I work 12 hours to get anything done. I still haven't learned that it balances out, and I feel guilty when I'm not working."

Then there's tradition again. We tend to remember all that our mothers did, and although common sense tells us that we're also holding down a job (mom probably wasn't), we still think we should be able to do everything at home as well as she did—and feel guilty if we don't.

Here's where Dr. Moss's trade-offs come in: If we're going to work, whether we have to or want to, we must begin to accept that there must be trade-offs, compromises, in every role that we accept as being within our standards.

Linda Koe, the Missouri banker, went back to work about five years ago and began the slow process of making and accepting trade-offs. "A lot of precedents had been set," she recalls. "The mother—me—always fixed the breakfast for everybody. The mother always did *everything*. For my husband, a lot of precedents had been set, too—the types of things that had been done for him. It was a real adjustment to switch everybody to another gear, that mother doesn't do everything anymore. I can't say that there is no guilt anymore. Early on, there was a lot. But I had reached the point where I *had* to do something for myself."

*Working Mother* magazine sent a questionnaire in 1979 entitled "How Has Working Changed Your Life?" to its readers; 2,000 responded. Although many of the respondents believed going to work had both financial and psychological benefits to them and their families, and many believed their families were aware of these advantages and felt no resentment toward the women for working, the women still felt guilty.

Readers were asked to list whatever they thought suffered as a result of their jobs: 70 percent answered housekeeping; 60 percent, time for themselves; 44 percent, their consciences, they didn't spend enough time with their families; 32 percent, the care of their children; 29 percent, their dispositions; 25 percent, the family's social life; 16 percent, their husband's comfort; 10 percent, their marriages.

## HOW WORKING CHANGES LIVES

Yet another question elicited positive, almost directly contradictory responses. When asked how working had changed their lives and those of their families, 66 percent said they felt more independent; 56 percent, happier; 39 percent, more energy; 63 percent, children more independent; 40 percent, children more helpful; 40 percent, husbands more helpful with housework and children.

The dichotomy is revealing. On one hand the women admit to the benefits to *both their families and themselves* of working; on the other, they insist on negating these good feelings with their guilt-stricken attitudes, even *knowing* that there's no reason for such feelings.

At this point, Dr. Moss's commonsense advice about coming to grips with guilt by just *coming to grips with it* can be extremely effective. Guilt is no longer something we're blissfully unaware of experiencing. It has come out of the closet. Yet, for whatever reasons, we insist on feeling guilty, even though we know better.

Worse, these feelings are transmitted to family members, so they may begin to believe we should be doing everything simply because *we* believe it!

If you're still unable to convince yourself that you have no reason to feel guilty as long as your priorities are straight, you've got company.

Gail Buchalter, a free-lance writer in Los Angeles and the separated mother of a three-year-old son, has tried various ways to arrange child care for Jordan, settling on a system that she feels is acceptable to her and the child. At the same time: "I feel extremely guilty because I don't know if I'm doing the best thing for my child. I think I'm doing the best thing for myself, but I don't know if it's going to be the best thing for him. I don't know if I should still be married and living in the mountains and being a full-time mother. It's hard to assign what's a responsibility and what's just ridiculous."

## HOW MOTHERS' WORKING AFFECTS CHILDREN

Child care is the biggest reason working mothers feel guilty, yet studies show this guilt is usually needless.

"Working mothers are more conscious of the time they spend with their children and use it more carefully than non-working mothers," observes Dr. Hugh Creedon, a psychologist with the Center for Family Studies at the Family Institute of Chicago. He also notes that women returning to work feel a sense of fulfillment that they transmit to their families. "It's important," he says, "for children to live in a home where people feel good about themselves."

Unlike the transmission of guilt to the family, the good feelings transmitted are a positive influence on everybody.

Psychologist Judith Bardwick confirms: "Studies of elementary-school children show that the best-adjusted children have a mother who is satisfied with what she's doing. Studies of adolescents have similar results. The attitude of the mother—whether she is pleased with what she is doing, or resentful, gratified or *guilty*—seems most important."

And Dr. Lois W. Hoffman, coeditor of *The Employed Mother in America,* concludes from various studies that "the working mother who obtains personal satisfaction from employment, *who does not have excessive guilt* and who has adequate household arrangements, is likely to perform as well as the nonworking mother, or better."

When women began going to work in large numbers, psychologists began studying the effects on the home, and the results should put working women's minds to rest. The main point to remember: If you're happy with your work and with the child-care arrangements, your contentment will register with the child and other family members.

Harriet Simpson, a newspaper editor in Belleville, Illinois, is also a divorced parent and mother of two sons, but with lots of experience at combining motherhood with working. She notes: "I've had periodic feelings of guilt about my going to work and leaving my sons. Now it's a way of life."

Another pervasive reason for guilt is that working women believe they're neglecting their husbands' comfort. The same *Working Mother* survey which showed that 16 percent of the respondents believed this also showed that only 10 percent of the husbands were opposed to having their wives work; 60 *percent* of the men were in favor of the idea. Although some men still oppose their wives working and do feel neglected, the situation is improving as working women become a way of life.

If husbands do not mind their wives working, even *like* their wives working, then they can probably get accustomed to not having all their needs catered to as before. For some it will take more time than others. For all it will involve good communication. But don't fight the fact that you're working by feeling guilty. Just as these feelings transmit to children, they also transmit to mates.

What has this got to do with time management? Only this: Guilt is a destructive force, and anything destructive will derail us from coping with our main priorities—which is one of the basic principles of time management.

*Guilt also is a major force in keeping us from taking time for ourselves.*

## RELAX! HOW?

Rosalie Davies, a musician and librarian in Safety Harbor, Florida, with three children (she's divorced), says, "I feel guilty when I sit around the house; I have a hard time relaxing in my own house, because there's always laundry that has to be done; and there's a screen in the back that has to be fixed because the dog got mad at me and chewed through it. I have hanging pots in my front vestibule, and one day the bottom of one just rotted out, and the pot and the plant fell. I walked around that for about five or six days just because I didn't have the energy to either pick it up or tell a child to pick it up. I feel real guilty about things like that."

Lawyer Laurie Hutzler, president of Legal Management Services in Manhattan, does work requiring her to watch a good deal of television. She still has twinges about it.

"I haven't been able to justify totally relaxing," says Ava Stern, publisher of *Enterprising Women,* a magazine for women entrepreneurs. "It must be guilt. If I'm not doing something constructive, that does it. I've got the very deep-seated American work ethic beaten into my head . . ."

"Most of the personal sights I set for myself do not get done," says insurance agent Karen Olson. "There's always something else competing with it. Somehow a commitment to anybody else is much more difficult to break. I feel guilty about breaking a commitment to somebody else. I don't feel guilty about breaking commitments to myself. I can always renegotiate with me—indefinitely."

Unless we get rid of guilt, we'll never be totally free to enjoy any time we might find for *ourselves.*

Guilt is the worst kind of time-waster. It leads to depression and other debilitating feelings. It also leads to us to try doing too much. It's an abuse of our time, certainly not an effective way of using it.

Liz Wolff, a teacher in Charlotte, North Carolina, and mother of three children, uses guilt as a warning signal:

"I do feel some guilt. But when I've overextended myself with work and mothering and car pooling and everything that you can get caught up in, that's when I usually stop to analyze my time: how I'm using it, what I don't need to do, and what I do need to do. I then eliminate what I can."

We'll show you how.

# Go Ahead: Say No!

If you want something done ask a busy person.

—ANONYMOUS

WE'VE ALL SAID YES when we're asked to do something and immediately regretted the decision, wishing we could blurt out what we really meant:

"No."

Many women find it practically impossible to say no. I find it to be one of my biggest handicaps in managing my own time. Although I'm working on it, I still sometimes find myself saying yes when I mean no and committing myself to projects or organizations that don't rank high on my priority list. The toll this takes is monumental.

A few years ago I became more and more involved with organizations outside (but related to) my business because I realized that one sign of the success of a business is to be visible. I started to give speeches and write articles; I became very active in the activities of the organizations I joined.

As I had intended, I became visible. So when the New York Association of Women Business Owners came up with the idea for a Women in Business Week, at the time the first in the country, uniting major corporations, small businesses, government agencies, and community associations into one week of activities free to the women of New York, they approached me with the proposal. I was, they assured me, the one person they knew who could organize such an event the way they visualized it. Flattery got them everywhere. I said yes.

It nearly killed me. I helped raise the money to fund the project, got all the printing done, organized the speakers and seminars—every detail, big and small, I handled it. The cost to me was unbelievable: my energy, my business, my personal life just went down the drain. It called for a lot of time management and good organizational skills. It was a product of what I can do and survive at great cost, but it was a job for Superwoman, and I would not recommend it to anybody in the world.

Next time . . . They approached me again. Again the flattery. Again I listened. But this time . . . "No!"

I had learned from my mistake and did not let my ego get the better of me. In the end I experienced the satisfaction of seeing ego triumph indirectly. When I said no, the organizers hired an entire public relations firm to accomplish the job I had done with the help of a handful of women volunteers.

My particular reason for hesitating to say no is guilt. I feel life has been very good to me. People have helped me. Now it's my turn to do my share. So when I'm asked to do things, it's still difficult for me to turn them down. I still find myself bogged down or overcommitted, but I'm improving rapidly!

## IT'S NOT RUDE!

Saying no is more of a problem for women than for men. The underlying cause is that we've been taught to be doers. We're always there to be supportive, to be helpmates. "No" is negative and therefore impolite. Right?

Wrong!

Many reasons tend to keep the word taboo. We feel that Super-women should never have to say no; they're supposedly capable of doing everything. We also want to be liked and appear co-operative; we're afraid of hurting someone else or putting that person in a bind; we may say yes because we think we'll be able to call on the other for a favor later, but not without having said yes in advance reciprocation; we may feel we "owe" it to the person asking.

Thousands of words have been written on this one little word. In time management, learning to say no is possible, perhaps not easily but surely with practice.

First, what are your own reasons for not being able to say no? And based on your list of priorities, what'll be your benefits if you do say no?

Usually the positive benefits far outweigh the anxieties of say-ing no. For example, if I'm asked to speak before a group, I should take a close look at my priorities before answering. If being visible or developing business contacts is still my A-1 priority, I may say yes with no regrets. If I had planned to spend that evening with a neglected friend, and *that's* my current priority, a no is in order.

It's much easier to do this sorting out if you have time, so don't be pressured into giving your yes or no answer on the spot. Sometimes, of course, you'll be able to see your priorities immediately, but frequently you'll need at least a few minutes to focus. Tell whoever is asking for your time that you'll get back, whether it's in five minutes or a week. Remember: Saying no takes practice.

At times it's not advisable to say no. If your boss asks you to do something, more than likely you should do it. But often you can say no graciously, and no one feels hurt or left in the lurch. Much depends on how you do it.

If a co-worker asks whether you have a minute to discuss something, an answer could be "No, I truly don't, but see me at 3:30 and we can discuss it then."

If a friend asks whether you could help with the rummage sale, an answer could be "No, I am busy that day, but Sally Jones may be interested. Have you called her?"

In the long run, the ability to say no will save you huge amounts of time and put you more at peace with yourself, since you can stop flogging yourself with that familiar cat-o'-nine-tails: "Life would be so much simpler, if only I'd said no."

Rosemary Gaillard, mother of two, has always been politically active in her community, Charlotte, North Carolina. When she went to work at a family service agency, her priorities immediately shifted. She decided her children were not going to get only leftover time, when she finished with work. So:

"I've gotten very good at saying no to whomever and whatever needs saying no to," says Gaillard. "I'm sure I'd feel guilty leaving the children—and the weeks that I'm busy, I do feel guilty. That's my signal that it's time to cut back and say no. I don't berate myself with guilt; it's just when I realize there've been too many things in a row that have been hectic, I start feeling it and see it in the children. Then I think, all right, time to pay attention! And I do."

## WHAT A RELIEF!

Instead of making you feel bad, saying no can actually make you feel much better in the long run than saying yes. Once you've gotten the difficult word out in situations that require it, there's an almost palpable feeling of relief, never that bitter twinge of regret a yes would have brought sooner or later.

One person we find it very easy to say no to is ourself. As Karen Olson noted in the previous section, we can always break commitments to ourselves because we don't have to answer to anyone else or worry about what anyone else will think when we're dealing silently and exclusively with ourselves.

*"No, I won't go to the beach today."*

*"No, I won't take that course in business administration."*

*"No, I won't go to the movie tonight."*

It's ever so easy to say no when it's to yourself!

Unfortunately, women are wrong when they think that not much happens when they say no to themselves. If you constantly deny yourself what you want or need to make room for everything and everybody else in your life, you're not only shortchanging yourself; you'll eventually shortchange everybody else too.

When you can't say no you wind up with overcommitment to people and projects, and that does you no good at all in the long term. You'll be frustrated with yourself and others with your seeming lack of time to do everything you had in mind.

That's why learning to say no, although painful and sometimes difficult, is one of the most important good deeds we can do for ourselves. It is, in fact, vital if we're to become good managers of our time.

Saying no is just part of the overall problem we women have with being assertive. Numerous books have been written on the subject, but for purposes of time management assertiveness is simply the ability to communicate your true wants, needs, and feelings to people to whom it matters.

Communication is an important tool in gaining control of your time and life. But, unless you take that first deep breath and say that first no or initiate that first air-clearing conversation with your family, co-worker, or friend, you're going to find your time used up by the demands of others and you'll never find time for yourself.

# How to Put a Price
# On Your Time

Women don't value their own time enough, don't put a high enough price on it, and don't insist that others pay that price if they want the time. Every minute wasted, whether you waste it yourself or allow others to waste it, is an opportunity lost to acquire a skill, earn money, think, plan, enjoy some well-deserved leisure.

— SYLVIA AUERBACH
*A Woman's Book of Money*

THE SAYINGS are so familiar that few of us stop to think what they mean:

*"Time is money."*

*"I'm buying time."*

Even when we do think about these truisms, very few of us are able to apply them to our lives, particularly in the home. Yet time is the most valuable commodity we've got. Literally. We even talk about it in the same terms as money:

*"Spend* your time (money) wisely, and you'll never regret what you've spent it on."

*"Invest* your time (money) well, and it'll pay off by giving you more time (money)."

"*Saving* time (money) is important for those crises (rainy days) when you can really use it."

We relate time to money when we talk (correctly) about people *stealing* our time. We adjust our schedules to the convenience of banks, repairmen, doctors, dentists, schools, husbands, businesses, children, family, and friends. Men have taken it for granted they will have uninterrupted blocks of time to do what needs to be done or what they want to do. Women, on the other hand, settle for bits of time they can fit around others' priorities. Women must begin to value their time.

Although we all realize how valuable time is and are always wishing we had more of it, when it comes right down to purchasing more time with money, we balk.

Why?

Here's why women have a mental block against paying for services or gadgets that would free up time:

1. Habit.
2. Economy.
3. Inability to put a price on our time.

## MEN DO IT BETTER

It's less often a mental block with our male counterparts. A single working man does not hesitate to have his laundry done or have a cleaning person in. A man embarking on his own business will hire a secretary almost before doing anything else. A man will delegate more because he sees the value of his time. Services in home and office free him up to get on to the important things: having fun, attracting new clients, or accomplishing more.

Habit keeps women, when in the same position, from using these services. We're so used to *doing* that we continue to do even when our activities reach such proportions that we become exhausted. The reason we hear most often for this is:

"I *can* do it, so I *do* do it."

Even while working on this book, after years of counseling women on the value of their time, I found myself fitting in the laundry between interviews on my Saturdays: Put the laundry in, do an interview; take the laundry out and put it in the drier, do a second interview; bring the laundry up . . .

I was so happy to be accomplishing two things at once (efficiency), I had forgotten I wasn't practicing what I preach. I blamed my tiredness at the end of this double duty on the interviews.

Finally a male friend said to me, "Diana, you're so busy telling all these other women to save wear and tear on themselves and to give themselves a free Saturday by having things like the laundry done, but you're not doing it yourself. What gives?"

## TIME EXPERT, HEAL THYSELF

Well, what gave was that like so many other women, I'd gotten so caught up in *doing* that I'd forgotten to *think*, to consider the options. It wasn't the money, it was habit.

I now drop my laundry off at a place around the corner from my apartment—and feel much better on Saturdays.

But habit runs even deeper than just feeling we should do

something because we can. It involves feeling *obligated* to do what we've been brought up to believe are woman's duties.

"Women have been conditioned," says Dr. Doris Moss. "They've been doing the laundry all those years, they think 'Why can't I handle it now?' I think they feel they're giving up some of their own authority."

Which means we're right back to the Superwoman syndrome: We feel that unless we do it all, we're failures.

"Women have internalized housekeeping roles so much," continues Dr. Moss, "that while moving on to new career roles they're still holding on to the old. If they're involved with a husband and children, maybe they don't want that place usurped by someone else. It's as if they've died, and the husband's gotten someone else in to take over their homemaking function. I got a sleep-in housekeeper and was working full-time when my kids were still home, and the housekeeper came down with rollers in her hair. My son said, 'Finally! A mother image,' which I thought was very funny. I wasn't the least bit threatened by the fact that this lady was in the house with rollers in her hair, doing all the work I didn't want to do in the first place."

Dr. Sarah Slagle agrees that tradition is keeping women from valuing their time:

"I'm sure much of this is simply learned behavior, parental expectations that have become so much a part of us we never question them. A study in Detroit a few years ago indicated that 87 percent of the female doctors questioned did all their own housework despite full-time professional commitments. I must say I find this hard to understand. I grew up in an atypical home for my day; my mother worked from the time I was five and even though by today's standards she did try to be Supermom by doing all her own work, her message to me for the most part was 'You've got studying to do.' So the housework expectation was not that strong. 'Have a neat house!' was strong, but it didn't matter if someone else did it, fortunately.

"When I first moved to New York and was working very long hours because of being in analytic training, I had only a studio apartment, but I hired someone to clean it and do my laundry. So I did value my time."

Then there's also guilt again! Hiring a housekeeper looks like a visible admission of our failure to meet society's standards. We rarely bother to remind ourselves that society's standards are hopelessly outdated for working women. Our paranoia is not unfounded, however. Society does tend to frown when a seemingly healthy young woman with a small apartment or house has the gall to bring in outside help. Maids, so tradition holds, are for the rich, not for the working class.

There's really only one reaction to this mass disapproval: To hell with what others think! It's your life, your mental health, and your free time that's at stake, not the rest of the world's.

## THIS HUSBAND HELPED

Susan Schwartz, a buyer for a large company in New York and mother of an infant, had household help even before the baby was born, because her husband urged her to do so.

"The whole idea of having somebody come to clean, even when we lived in a one-bedroom apartment, was ridiculous to me. My husband would ask me why I didn't hire somebody." They had a precedent: "With yard cleaning around the house, neither he nor I wanted to do it, so once a year we called somebody to do it. Our feeling is as long as we can afford it, why should we give our free time to be with each other and the baby when we don't have to?"

Again, it was a man who saw the benefits of hiring a service rather than doing it yourself. Schwartz's happy ending is, of course, that paying for services to save her time has become habitual.

We emphasize paying for housekeeping services because many women have serious trouble accepting alternatives. But the *time is money* principle applies to many opportunities for buying yourself time in the home and at the office by paying for services and products. Consider:

Services for the office include management consultants, marketing consultants, public relations firms, personnel consultants, lawyers, accountants, bankers, financial consultants, typists.

Office products include copy machines rather than carbons, self-erasing typewriters, office computers (word processors) . . .

Computers?

"I really debated about this," says Laurie Hutzler. "Word processors cost a lot of money, but then, I do a lot of writing. And it's already paid off in time and headaches saved."

Services for the home include laundry, housekeeper, ironing, window washers, rug and upholstery cleaners, shopping services (food and clothes), child-care services, diaper service, milk and other delivery services, shopping by phone and mail order.

Time-saving home products include dishwashers, washer and drier, crock pot, microwave oven, self-cleaning oven, and self-defrosting refrigerator.

Schwartz pinpointed the second reason women don't pay for more services or time-saving devices ". . . as long as we can afford it." Sometimes personal financial situations just don't allow us to hire a housekeeper or purchase a microwave oven. This is a lot less simple to dismiss with a wave of the hand than society's frowns.

Single mothers in particular cite tight budgets as reason for not paying for more services. Often the child-support check doesn't arrive, much less pay the bills it takes to raise children, keep up the mortgage payments, and pay for transportation.

What to do then? Take time to check out your spending priorities; weigh what you're doing now against the potential of more disposable time and what that time could do for you.

## TRADING MONEY FOR TIME

Could the money you're spending on cigarettes or liquor or other nonessentials be used to hire a housekeeper part-time? If so, would the sacrifice be worth the four-or-so extra hours you'd have on Saturday with your children or by yourself?

Is the initial investment of a few dollars for an extra-long telephone cord worth the future time it will give you by permitting you to talk on the phone and work around the house at the same time?

Instead of full-time household help, perhaps at least twice a year you can hire someone to do the heavy duty work: windows, carpets, floors, oven. It makes a great birthday or Christmas present, either to give or to get.

Big or small, these financial decisions are very personal and we can't make them for you. Your own priorities should be carefully considered, however, when it comes to spending money versus saving time, and if you can see where cutting corners monetarily will build up your time account, then perhaps you should try it, even if it's only on an experimental basis.

Priorities help in another way too, with more long-run effects. If you absolutely cannot afford any services now, and if your priorities are other than such services, setting *goals* to eventually hire help can clarify future priorities, bringing them a little closer because you're not working toward some vague, undefined "tomorrow."

Setting such a goal can also make it a bit easier to "dabble," as we'll discuss later—to take the first baby step to attaining a goal.

Newspaper editor Harriet Simpson looks at it this way:

"My time is valuable. That's why I started taking my laundry out. It's worth more than it's costing me to sit there and watch the drier. That's one of the luxuries I allowed myself. I do have someone come in four hours every two weeks. It just happens that's all I could get her, and all I could really afford. So that's great. I don't have to mop floors anymore."

Many women have shared similar experiences. Unable to afford full-time housekeeping help, they're getting started by hiring just as much as they can afford at this time. The results strengthen their determination to get full-time help just as soon as finances allow, and it's a good way to experiment to see if housekeeping help is what you need.

There's another way to fudge the "can't afford it" problem, a way that's increasing in popularity to such an extent that the Internal Revenue Service is even nosing into it: *barter.*

## HOW TO BARTER

Barter may be tricky or sometimes difficult to set up. It has worked for many people who barter skills, products, and time for something they need or want.

One of the most common forms of bartering used by many working mothers is the baby-sitting co-op. Although this is a barter of time, and you're not really *saving* any time since you're expected to pay it back, what you are doing is *restructuring* your time to better suit you. Restructuring—or investing—time is just as important as saving time because it enables you to use that time more effectively.

For example, if you can count on a member of your sitting co-op to take your child Tuesday night, giving you a chance to work or go to a movie, you'll be much more relaxed when it comes time for you to take her children. This holds true in any form of barter of services. Perhaps you enjoy sewing and can offer to make an attorney friend's clothes in return for her legal advice.

The combinations are limitless: service for service, product for service, product for product. The main thing to remember is: Don't get so enthusiastic that you outsmart yourself and start trading off *too much* of your time.

Cheryl Hughes, an independent consultant for a firm in Los Angeles and a mother, admits she "lives in fear" of her daughter becoming ill. She's taken steps in advance to ease the fear:

"When she's not too sick, I have arranged an awful lot of bartering with my friends, so I do have someone to call on. I have a friend, an artist, who's starting up a business. She's very talented, but she did not really have the business sense to get going on the line of furniture she's marketing. So I spent a couple of days with her saying 'Here's what you should do now and what you should do next,' because I had the training in that area.

"In return, she is now giving me help with child care, car pooling, and that sort of thing, which is what *I* need. I had to give a dinner party recently at the end of a very long day, and I could not prepare for it. So in exchange for using the swimming pool, another friend set up my dinner party for me. I guess the bartering sort of happened and then I realized what was going on. We just casually say, 'Oh, can you help me?' and it builds. We've got a real network going and it's fantastic."

Although approaching somebody with the initial idea may be difficult, many people have found others to be delighted with the idea of bartering goods and services rather than paying for them or being paid. It's a viable solution to the problem of women with tight budgets who would like to hire some help.

# IS THIS PENNY REALLY NECESSARY?

We have to ask ourselves if sometimes our penny pinching is more false economy than financial necessity.

I once heard of a woman who'd read that a supermarket was having a sale on macaroni. She arrived home from work, fetched a neighbor, hopped a train to Hoboken, New Jersey (she lived in Manhattan), walked ten minutes from the train station to the market, bought two boxes of macaroni *and* two sacks full of other groceries that were not on sale, struggled back to the train station with her heavy bags, returned home.

The trip took nearly three hours. It cost her sixty cents round trip on the train. The two bags of groceries cost an additional $30. She *saved* 20 cents on two boxes of macaroni—ten cents off each box.

This story may be an extreme—but unfortunately, it's true, and it's an excellent illustration of false economy: *We become so intent on saving money that we don't realize that the time we're spending—or even additional money—totally negates the initial savings.*

More common than our macaroni example is the woman who—knowing she can do the typing and filing—doesn't hire a secretary, so she can save money. What happens? She becomes so involved in secretarial details that she *loses* money because she's unable to go after new clients or find time to resolve recurring problems in the office.

At home, it's more difficult to see this time-as-money relationship to household services, because we're unable to place a value on our time. Ava Stern, publisher of *Enterprising Women,* has conducted numerous studies of businesswomen and found that the inability to place a price tag on time is general:

"Women tend to be so delighted that they can do something and so used to having their services unpaid for that they tend to undervalue themselves; the doing is the reward itself. So money is a low priority. The accomplishment, the sense of achievement is more of a reward than the monetary reward. Men say very pragmatically, 'We're going to make a million-dollar profit this year or we're not going into business.' Women very rarely do that until they've been in business ten years . . ."

If women have this much trouble equating time spent at work (for which they get paid) with money, it's understandable why they cannot see that their time at home (for which they don't get paid) is also valuable.

## WHAT ARE YOU WORTH PER HOUR?

Karen Olson has devised a nuts-and-bolts system that places a monetary value on each hour she spends at work:

"I instinctively will not spend a half hour having a personal discussion with somebody during the business day, because I point out to myself that I just cost myself $50. I charge myself high. In reality, I'm not yet using my time well enough so that I should be charging myself at $100 an hour. But I surtax it just so that I'm impressed."

Olson instituted this system when she became impressed with the undeniable fact that in a business time *is* money. So she asked herself, "OK, how much money is ten minutes?" But how about at home?

"Money," she says, "is an easy unit of measure to use. Now what is time equivalent to at home? Equivalent to satisfaction or rest or enjoyment? There's no handy unit of measurement. To come up with a calorie or an ounce or a centimeter of happiness is kind of hard."

We suggest that you keep reminding yourself: *Time is valuable!* At home that'll work better than *time is money*.

One reason we don't recognize our time at home as valuable is, obviously, that nobody else ever has. Housewives have never gotten paid for their work, so with today's emphasis on money the implication is that housework is worthless.

Only in 1979 have efforts been made to place a monetary value on a homemaker's time, and as columnist Sylvia Porter noted, even that is "a most conservative estimate; in fact, so understated that it's nonsense."

The estimates put the full-time homemaker's work week at 99.6 hours and the pay, figured on minimum wage levels of the late seventies, at $362.71 a week, or $18,862.48 a year. The Census Bureau arrived at even lower wages—$15,952 annually before taxes.

Despite the low figures, it's significant that women's work in the house is finally being assigned some dollar value. Even more important, women themselves need to put a price on their time, rather than continuing to devalue it. Think of it this way:

A Saturday with our children is worth the $30 it costs to have a housekeeper one weekday per week.

Twenty dollars is a small price to pay for a crock pot that'll enable you to put dinner on in the morning and go to the beach for the rest of the day (restructures, rather than saves, time).

Ten dollars a week for laundry services is more than reasonable, considering it relieves us from having to stay by the washer and drier when we'd rather be doing something else.

If we can afford such services, we should recognize that these prices *are* relatively small when it comes to our mental health.

Linda Koe observes: "I do pay to have things done for me because that allows me to do some of the things that I want to do. I have a male housekeeper. I would kill to keep him. He does everything, including windows. Besides the cleaning, he does errands—grocery shopping, laundry, picking up my dry cleaning, picking up pictures at the camera store, all of that, which just frees up a whole chunk of time . . . He *is* my wife. He saves my sanity."

*When we buy our time, we're buying our mental health.*

## WHAT'S SANITY WORTH?

Dr. Sarah Slagle notes: "I find myself many times each week questioning women why they feel they have to be Superwoman and urging, where they can afford it at all, that they have some household help. Often, for the amount of money a professional woman can earn in three hours—and it probably takes her ten to clean the house and do the laundry—she can hire somebody to do it. She'll save time and energy that can better be spent on other things—such as time with her family."

Every woman I know, without exception, who currently has household help or makes use of time-saving ideas, recommends it without qualification to anyone who isn't already doing so. The consensus is: "It frees me up to have fun, to do things I want to do."

Vicki Riker, media director for an in-house advertising agency and divorced mother of two daughters, expresses the exuberance of freedom that household help gives these women: "It frees me from having to do all that crap! I can go and read; I can go out; my Saturday's free. Yippee! Just having a Saturday, to go do what I want to do without having to be concerned [with a dirty house] is terrific. Saturdays, I'm taking ballet lessons. I'm painting. I wish I'd done it before."

Rosemary Gaillard, no less enthusiastic, adds: "I've had a baby-sitter who comes and helps keep up the house and I've had a baby-sitter who just comes in and takes care of the children; I prefer the former. It costs more, but it relieves me from having to worry about washing socks. If someone, while they're here taking care of the children (they don't require that much minute-by-minute attention) will throw the laundry in, I'm willing to pay for that. It alleviates a lot of stress. *I am buying my own time—and it's worth it.*"

# The Blessings of Networking

I think women tend to be afraid that it's a terrible thing to take advantage of supportive systems. Mother didn't have supportive systems, so they must be something terrible; [women] fail to realize that the only way men have ever survived is that they've had supportive systems . . .

—CAROL BELLAMY
*President, New York City Council*

IN 1977 Jane Wilson wrote what came to be regarded as the definitive article on "New Girl Networking." It was also one of the first to discuss the profitability of career women forming networks mostly to find out what's happening on the business scene.

The article was a galvanizing force. It pushed women from tentative steps toward networking to making major strides. It also put a name to something that, left unnamed, is merely an informal way of making and using contacts. "Networking" immediately began to take on elitist connotations. Clubs were formed and rules were made to such an extent that many women became confused and intimidated by the term, which is unfortunate; networking is a valuable tool for saving time and advancing your career.

Three years after her first article, Wilson reviewed the growth of networking, noting the exclusivity of some of the organizations and putting her finger on exactly what networking is:

"The first requirement for network membership is more or less naked self-interest—and this for many women is something new. Each link in a career network unapologetically exploits her contacts within the group on a loose quid pro quo basis. Until recently, women have not developed the usable, pragmatic relationships that men have always maintained without apparent moral uneasiness. Self-esteem is a prerequisite. To make use of others, you need to feel usable yourself."

## HOW IT WORKED FOR DIANA

Networking has probably been one of the biggest time- and money-savers in my career and personal life. It needn't be done in a formal group or organization; you can do it on the phone or while having lunch with a few friends.

Through my network contacts, I found a job (before starting my own business); hired employees for my business; found office space; obtained assistance on projects I was working on; got many of my clients.

In my personal life, I have found my present apartment through the network; located a kennel for my dog, Jolly; gotten some of my "best buys" through contacts.

When I have a need for something, I "put out the word" to my friends and contacts. Within a few days I get calls recommending people or places, whatever I asked for. In return, I often receive calls from people asking for my help. I've always found people willing to help me *but only if I ask for that help.* They're as busy as I am and nobody has time to wait on street corners to toss goodies at you. So do ask! In return, my networkers know I'll do the same if I have information they need. Everybody saves enormous amounts of time.

However you choose to make use of a networking system

whether by joining formal organizations or informally keeping your ear to the ground, remember:

Networking provides access to information that will make your job easier in innumerable ways: knowledge of what jobs are available, new rules and regulations applicable to women, contacts needed to get a particular job done—anything and everything on a "need to know" basis.

You gain time because you can turn to people who have either done it before or know where to tell you to turn for assistance, so you don't have to start from the bottom and from scratch.

*There's no sense in reinventing the wheel, right?*

Why do so many women feel that unless they do it *all by themselves,* even though it's been done before, they're not doing an adequate job? Why *do* they reinvent the wheel over and over again?

It's a fact that women hesitate to make use of contacts. They feel it's asking a favor they "shouldn't" be asking; they feel they're admitting an inadequacy because they even need to ask; they feel it's *using* people, and, in turn, they do not want to be used back; and, of course, they feel that unless they do it all by themselves, they're not the Superwomen they think they should be.

Women don't realize, as Carol Bellamy, Jane Wilson and others keep pointing out, that men have always made use of the network system. They had access to it in the office, on the golf course, at the end of a day over a drink before going home, at the men's club. Women knew how it was being done; they just did not have the same access.

## ITS MANY MALE USES

Since men have had more experience at networking (they never gave it a name, by the way; women invented the phrase "good ole boys' network"), they're more effective at it. They make use of contacts without hesitation, guilt, embarrassment. Here's how:

Need to know whom to contact at a certain magazine to pitch an article to? Call John Smith; he's had many articles published in the magazine. (Three years later John Smith may call back to find out who your lawyer is who did such a great job on the book contract.)

Want to buy a house and you're not clear about the procedure, having been an apartment dweller your whole life? Call Jane Doe; her father's a realtor.

Writing a proposal on nursing home administrative pointers? Call Bob Jones whom you met at a cocktail party last month and who happens to be deputy administrator for a private home.

Whatever your need, there's bound to be someone around who, even if unable to give specific help, can point you in the right direction, saving you many frustrating steps of starting without leads.

Networking comes in many guises and formal organizations frequently make it easier to use. Such organizations aren't all elitist. One of the most productive groups I've ever joined is the New York Association of Women Business Owners. At our meetings we learn formally what's going on in business and informally keep tabs on people, events, developments. From making contacts to conducting seminars, the group provides invaluable aid to women in business.

Even women who're aware of the value of establishing good contacts may overlook some excellent ways to encounter and connect with such contacts, particularly when these pop up outside formal "approved" networking systems. The many guises of networking include informal systems that are just as effective as membership in organizations.

When I set up Women in Business Week I scheduled special luncheons with representatives from major corporations for every day of the week. At one of the organizational meetings some of the other women wondered aloud why I had done so, joking that it was because "Diana likes to eat."

"Here you are always complaining that you don't have access to these people," I told them, "and I set up luncheons where you can informally meet *all of them,* an opportunity to hand out your business cards, talk about your business and make contacts. Attending both the luncheons and the cocktail parties can be the most important time you spend this week! You'll meet people informally. It may seem worthless at the time, but *later* when you call, they'll remember meeting you and the doors will open."

Still skeptical, the women agreed to the luncheons and everyone attended. Years later, I'm still hearing how that was one of the most valuable lectures I ever gave. The women find that doors have opened.

Another program I have participated in is an annual event, "Contact—A Conference for Businesswomen," sponsored by the YWCA of New York City. At this event, we feature programs such as "Mentor Relationships," "The New Networks," and "Making and Taking Opportunities." The purpose is to expose women to the opportunities men in business have always had and been using all along.

Linda Koe recognizes the career-helping as well as the time-saving benefits of networking:

"I'm involved in a project right now at work in which I am to be the hospital industry representative and I have to be as expert as I can on the hospital industry and what banking services we might offer. That will be my specialty. One of my very good friends sells IBM equipment to hospitals; she's in every hospital in this town. I'll be able to talk to her about that and get background from her. Another woman I know is involved with the hospital association. All I have to do is pick up the phone to get what I need."

## AND NOW FOR YOUR OWN TEAM!

*Teamwork* is another way of looking at networking. We're all aware how males look at their business world as "one big team" and that they all are (or are supposed to be) "team players." Again, women have shortchanged themselves. They seem determined to strike out on their own. We don't want to do *everything* the way men have been doing for years. But where's the payoff? Although individualism is admirable, when it begins to affect your effectiveness it seems pretty pointless.

Networking, like barter, can take many interesting turns. Just as you must be willing to make use of contacts, you must be willing to be available as a contact, which is where Wilson's emphasis on the need for self-esteem comes in. You must believe you have something to offer, not necessarily in direct, proportional repayment value, but something of value. And everybody does. *Everybody.*

Look at Cheryl Hughes's trade-off in the previous section: child care and car pooling for Hughes's expertise in marketing—barter, the result of networking.

And Rosemary Gaillard, who works at a family service agency, is just one of many women who have found baby-sitters through network contacts.

Teacher Liz Wolff has found an additional time-saving benefit of belonging to a woman's group:

"I've been involved with a women's group for about two years and in that relationship of eight women we've gotten to know each other really well. We have asked support from women in the group in areas that we know we need work on, and by this time we know each other and know each other's needs and continually get feedback. [It saves time] in lots of ways.

"When I'm there, it sort of concentrates my evaluations of things and the feedback from my friends. Also I have seven intimate relationships in one weekly time frame. It sounds pretty structured, but it's really functional for me because for me to have a three-hour conversation with one person compared to seven people with feedback and support—there's no comparison. I don't have time for seven intimate friends, and yet I do have seven intimate friends."

Do think of this all as networking. That helps define it for those who have trouble recognizing the system and its value. Our examples illustrate how *unlimited* such networking and its values can be. From business contacts to barter . . . to keeping track of friends; from business contacts to friendship contacts . . . the guises are truly limitless. You'd do well to be constantly on the lookout for ways to plug into your personal network. You work for it, it works for you. All in minimum time.

# Planning: Using the Master Key

By failing to plan, you are planning to fail.
—R. ALEC MACKENZIE
*The Time Trap*

Prior planning prevents poor performance.
—ANONYMOUS

THE MASTER KEY to effective time management, as we've said, is planning. From an overall life plan right down to the nitty-gritty of each day, specific plans can add hours to a 24-hour day if you're practical and realistic. You may object:

*"If I don't have enough time to begin with, where will I get the time to plan?"*

*"I can plan—I just can't carry out those plans."*

*"Planning takes the spontaneity out of living."*

First things first. The time log in the next section will help you find the few extra minutes you need to do your planning. Initially, it'll be difficult to establish the new habits that will give you this time. But since those few minutes are all you'll need to save time, energy, and headaches, they're important minutes to find. You can!

About not being able to carry out those plans once they're

made: Too many people set such unrealistic goals for themselves that it's impossible to accomplish everything, so frustration sets in and the plans are abandoned. Some women realize this, but most can't understand what went wrong.

"In my business," says Ava Stern, "I've always assumed I could do the impossible in a month, something that might normally take six months to a year. It's caused me a lot of problems. It's like my eyes are bigger than my stomach. I have begun to understand the reality of time, how long things really do take."

Newspaper editor Harriet Simpson, on the other hand, despairs that "I never seem to be able to plan my life in such a way that I have time for all the things I want to do. Planning is one thing; executing those plans is something else."

Simpson realizes that her main problem is "getting bogged down, trying to do too much, but also failing in terms of setting and adhering to priorities. I tend to make a pretty good plan, and it looks good on paper, then the child will fall down the stairs . . ."

People set unrealistic goals for all kinds of reasons: They may actually believe they can do it all. They may feel they're *expected* to be able to do it all. *They may simply not take into account the possibility of such a crisis as the child falling down the stairs.* Which brings us to the third and most challenging problem people have with planning: allowing for spontaneity through flexibility.

If planning is realistic to begin with, flexible time should be built in. Planning doesn't make life less spontaneous! It's intended to make spontaneity much more enjoyable because things are generally running smoothly. It's anything *but* a taskmaster. It's a liberator.

Just as planning is the key to time management, so is flexibility the key to good planning. Whether it's planning your life or planning your day, you must remember to allow for changes and crises. You can allow for flexible time (a little extra leeway to deal with the unexpected). And you can maintain flexible mental attitudes and permit yourself to change your mind and reevaluate priorities.

## WHY IT'S THE ONLY WAY

This may sound morbid, but I, for one, don't want to wake up one day and find I'm being carried off into the wild blue yonder shouting, "Whoa, I still have something else to do!" I want to be able to say peacefully, "I'm ready, I did it all. I'm happy with my life."

And the only way I can do that is to start specifically to plan out my life and how I'm going to go about doing this planning. First should come the life plan, the quality-of-life values I want (which we will detail later). Second—how I'm going to achieve the overall plan—is what makes up my days, and that's what we'll talk about now: the big and little activities that become the stairway to my life plan.

The *only* way you can get what you want is to plan for it, again with flexibility built in. I am planning my life, *knowing* as I get older my plans are going to change, because *I'm* going to grow and evolve. But at least I have set my targets on something and am actively working toward achieving that something.

It's ironic that women should have a problem with planning, because women have a definite knack for it. In fact, it would be fair to say women can plan rings around their male counterparts.

It all goes back to that mixed blessing-curse: tradition. Women are probably the most experienced at planning because they've had to do much of it throughout their lives: planning meals, planning the children's education, planning the weekend outings.

And these planning abilities are synonymous with organization. Let's look at some traditional situations:

Most political candidates have had women in the back office planning their activities.

Women have planned and executed the smooth running of offices, ensuring that executives have everything running smoothly, both in their absence and their presence.

Women have always planned activities for service-related organizations: clubs, church groups, social groups.

Women have planned the operation of the home, dinner parties, coordinating housework, preparation of meals, etc.

Women have planned the needs of their children, the economics of their home, the needs of their husbands.

With this extensive background in planning details, why do we as women resist the idea of planning our lives? It's apparent from the above list that most functions for which women have served as the chief planners have placed them in a subordinate role. We plan, all right, but almost always for others, usually men. We do the basic planning, but have *never assumed the ultimate responsibility.*

For example, that carefully scheduled political candidate has the responsibility to follow that schedule and win; the boss, not his secretary, has the responsibility to look over her work—and it's his Mercedes on the line, not hers.

Susan Friedman, a mother and a doctor's secretary at a Brooklyn hospital, verbalizes the frustrations inherent in such a relationship:

"Since I'm a secretary, the doctors and administrators will not acknowledge my existence, so what happens is I have to work alone for two or three days on a pile of things and then I'll have to force my boss to sit down with me and go over every single piece of paper before it leaves the office. I cannot take the chance of his not being aware of it."

So the planner, who bird-dogs the details, the delays, frustrations, obstacles, misunderstandings, and other headaches, frequently never even sees the end result of her careful plan. And if she sees the results, she generally is not credited for finessing it all.

That's why women have a major problem applying their planning skills to a truly responsible career. And that's why so many housewives wishing to reenter the job market seek career guidance. They need someone to assure them that their skills, for so long belittled or taken for granted, are actually worth money.

## WHY WOMEN ARE SHORTCHANGED

The two basic reasons for our inability to use our talent, from planning a party to planning work in business, are:

1. *Women have been made to feel inferior.* The message has been: Stay home, honey, raise the children, and leave business and *hard work* to us men. (Raising children *isn't* hard work? The implication, of course, is that it's not.)

2. *Cultural differences have seen to it that women have been denied responsibility.* Responsibility is therefore an unfamiliar entity, and so many women are afraid of it. They're in awe of the men who make decisions; they feel comfortable *only* at planning and leaving the ultimate responsibility to the Men-Who-Know-How.

At the risk of sounding simplistic: There is no myth or mystery about planning for yourself instead of others.

*Just do it!*

Set a goal and then develop a method of achieving that goal. Whether it's baking a cake or making vice-president at your bank, the routine is the same:

1. Set a goal.
2. Decide on the steps needed to achieve the goal.
3. Establish priorities for the steps.
4. Set schedules, timetables, deadlines.

Back to the original problem, then: Where do you get this time to plan for yourself?

First you have to know where your time is going now. Once you know that, which we'll shortly show you with the time log, then you—and *only* you—must decide where your time should be going. Some of it, obviously, should be going to planning. *Plan time to plan.*

# *Your Time Log Tells All*

---

THE TIME LOG, we'll admit right off, is the most tedious step on the route to good planning. It's also one of the most helpful. Fortunately, it's usually a one-time, one-week affair and then it's over with. That's not a bad trade for a lifetime of time control, is it?

The log is simply a list of your daily activities, preferably recorded in 15-minute intervals, and it's long been used as an effective tool in business. Its priceless value in time management is that it shows us precisely what our *real time-robbers* are, at the office and at home. Once you know what these robbers are, you can begin a campaign to eliminate or change them. Presto: you're freeing up bits and pieces or whole chunks of previously wasted time.

You probably think you already know how you're wasting time, that the log will merely confirm the obvious. But you may be in for a big surprise—I was!

As I've mentioned, I've always been extremely *efficient*. My organizational abilities were, in fact, what prompted me to go into the business of, originally, setting up offices for other companies.

So why, if I was so efficient, was I working 18 hours a day, seven days a week? I started asking myself what I was doing it all for. I thought I was going to have fun and at the same time earn a fairly decent income and be creative, not turn into a business-mad drudge.

It took about two years before I started to scream for help. I sat down and thought about it, and said, "Hey, you, if you're always being hired for your organizational abilities and pride yourself on being the quickest in thinking of the easy way, how can you screw up your life for yourself?" That's when I turned to time management for help and learned that efficient isn't necessarily effective.

## YOU CAN'T DO EVERYTHING

What had been killing me was that I had been doing *every-thing*—nice and fast, to be sure—but still everything, and that's impossible. At least if you want to reach your main goals.

It was my time log that made me see how a lot of the *everything* I was doing was merely robbing me of my time, rather than helping me achieve the goals I had set.

Among other things, my time log showed me I was opening and answering mail that didn't contribute to my business; I was returning too many phone calls that I could spot as unimportant before I ever made them; I was in short, letting small details keep me busy and away from the important tasks that would make my business successful.

Your time log will show you something different, since each time log is as personal as an individual's biorhythm. But each time log will show you where your time goes.

Where *does* our time go? Most of us don't really know, though we may think we do. We certainly know that we're tired at the end of the day; that we've been going for what seems like 48 hours, answering questions, shuffling papers, writing reports, washing dishes, cleaning closets . . . And yet, and yet: how much time do we really spend on each of these activities? Ask yourself: "Am I really doing more than I think or am I really doing less than I think and working too hard at it?"

The Time Log knows.

So don't procrastinate. Pick a week, grit your teeth, and start marking time. The little extra work will pay off. We know a lot of women who analyzed their time and found that it paid off for them:

Independent consultant Cheryl Hughes found she was spending a lot of time driving to meet clients who lived in various directions from her office. Sometimes she broke up an entire day to meet one client. She began organizing her time so she could meet on specific days with several clients who all lived in the same part of town. This left her two free days for office work that had been suffering. "It's much more sane," reports Hughes.

Teacher Liz Wolff analyzes her time whenever she gets frustrated. Results? She found time to exercise; she found it permissible to "waste" 15 to 20 minutes in the morning reading the newspaper and drinking coffee; she realized that she could get her children to help her, at the same time giving her more time and the children a sense of responsibility. She still automatically analyzes her time whenever she finds herself facing another "systems overload."

Karen Olson, the insurance agent, in her effort to "stop the merry-go-round" kept a telephone log for a while. Her complete record of incoming and outgoing calls enable her to manage her time on the telephone a lot more rationally:

". . . If a call starts wandering into somebody spending 20 minutes on a personal discussion, I either tell them I don't have time right now, that I have to get out of the office in two minutes—whether I do or not—or that I have to take another call. Only once or twice a year is somebody an absolute bulldog; my hints are usually enough of a signal for almost anybody who's civilized."

Rosalie Davies, a musician and librarian, also kept a time log at work "to see where we were spending our time, because we felt that we weren't doing anything. Every time the phone rang or every time someone came in or every time someone wanted something . . . I'd write it down. And sure enough, at the end of the day—no wonder I was tired!"

Davies' log pinpointed the "minor" activities that had built up to an exhausting level. Aware of them now, she is able to minimize these time and energy robbers.

Although we don't suggest keeping a log for more than one week, you should definitely do it for more than a few days, because the days you choose may not be typical in your life.

## TIME-LOG TRAPS

Avoid these pitfalls in keeping a time log:

1. Waiting and trusting your memory until the end of the day to complete the log.
2. Not being precise in marking down what you're doing.

Regarding the first, can we really remember at the end of the day *everything* we did? That's the main problem, after all: Most of us do so much, and get so involved in so many details that we aren't fully conscious of what we're doing; that is, how we're spending the time.

It's much more accurate and profitable to record your log in 15-minute increments as you do what you're doing.

As for leaving out details, they're anything but trivial! It's the very details that kill our time. Putting down "Telephone call 10:15" will do absolutely nothing for you. You must be sure to note who called, the purpose of the call, length of the call, resulting action, if any, etc.

These details are crucial when it comes time to reap the rewards of your time log. A well-kept log will reveal well-kept personal secrets to you. Take a long look at every item, every activity. If the activity was a phone call, ask yourself: Was a large part of the call unnecessary? Could it have been cut off (gracefully)? Was the resulting action a priority task or busywork? How could it have been better handled? Could it have been delegated? Could you have said no? Go through a similar follow-up for each activity.

Obviously, the time log is an important prelude to discovering the crux of your own problems with time. Don't just keep the log in the office, either. A detailed log should also be kept at home, both mornings and evenings, so that eventually you can create a home life that will run as smoothly as your office.

The time-*robbers* will often be different in the home than at work; yet sometimes you'll find a remarkable correlation. Essentially they all boil down to the same: loss of valuable minutes that can be put to much better use as time-*savers*—once you've found the little robbers.

1. Note the time an activity took place.
2. Describe the activity.
3. Note whether the activity was planned, a priority, or an interruption.
4. Note who the activity involved.

5. Mark down thinking time, daydreaming, everything.
6. Analyze time log at the end of the day for:
   —Time-wasters.
   —How you can resolve them.

Since "time is cumulative," this process of saving a few minutes here and a few minutes there is what will ultimately put many more hours back into your life. (Sample time sheets follow.)

# DAILY TIME SHEET

### TIME FOR ME

| TIME | ACTIVITY | Planned | Interrupt | Priority | INVOLVED WITH | COMMENT |
|------|----------|---------|-----------|----------|---------------|---------|
| 8:00 a.m. | Cooked breakfast | ✓ | | | Alone | Could delegate to children |
| 8:15 a.m. | Searched for bank statement | | ✓ | | Husband | Set up system |
| 8:30 a.m. | Dressed for work | ✓ | | ✓ | Alone | Plan ahead |
| 8:40 a.m. | Stop at shoemaker | ✓ | | | Alone | Could delega |
| 9:15 a.m. | Start preparation of sales forecast | ✓ | | ✓ | Secretary | |
| 9:20 a.m. | Phone call – J. Jones – Re: mtg. | | ✓ | | Caller J.J. | |
| 9:25 a.m. | Sales forecast – work started again | ✓ | | ✓ | Secretary | |
| 9:40 a.m. | Visitor – salesperson for new equipment | | ✓ | | Visitor | Should have set an appt. |
| 10:30 a.m. | Write ltr. to M. Smith – results of mtg. | ✓ | | | Alone | Don't have file ready |
| 11:00 a.m. | Phone call – Janet – social call | | ✓ | | Alone | Took too long |
| 11:30 a.m. | Mtg. – planning session – Mgt. team | ✓ | | ✓ | Mgt. team | Could have been better planned |
| 1:30 p.m. | Rush job for client x – not happy | | ✓ | | J.B.M. | Crisis |
| 2:45 p.m. | Phone call – problem w/ prod. dept. | | ✓ | | M.S. | Plan better |
| 4:00 p.m. | Review proposal from S.J. Write ltr. | ✓ | | | alone | Wasn't planned |
| 5:30 p.m. | Buy groceries for dinner | ✓ | | | Alone | |

### TIME WASTERS—CAUSE / SOLUTION

| TIME WASTERS—CAUSE | SOLUTION |
|--------------------|----------|
| Breakfast prep took too long | Delegate to teenager or plan ahead for easier cooking methods |
| Searching for bank statement | Set up filing system |
| Interruption on sales forecast | Tell secy not to be interrupted for 1 hour |
| Phone calls – too many repeat callers | Delegate to secy to screen calls |
| Drop-in visitor | No open-door policy |
| Crisis | Anticipate possible problem areas |
| Groceries | Could have been preordered and delivered |

## DAILY TIME SHEET

TIME FOR ME

| TIME | ACTIVITY | Planned | Interrupt | Priority | INVOLVED WITH | COMMENT |
|------|----------|---------|-----------|----------|---------------|---------|
|      |          |         |           |          |               |         |
|      |          |         |           |          |               |         |
|      |          |         |           |          |               |         |
|      |          |         |           |          |               |         |
|      |          |         |           |          |               |         |
|      |          |         |           |          |               |         |
|      |          |         |           |          |               |         |
|      |          |         |           |          |               |         |
|      |          |         |           |          |               |         |
|      |          |         |           |          |               |         |
|      |          |         |           |          |               |         |
|      |          |         |           |          |               |         |
|      |          |         |           |          |               |         |
|      |          |         |           |          |               |         |
|      |          |         |           |          |               |         |
|      |          |         |           |          |               |         |

| TIME WASTERS—CAUSE | SOLUTION |
|--------------------|----------|
|                    |          |
|                    |          |
|                    |          |
|                    |          |
|                    |          |
|                    |          |
|                    |          |
|                    |          |
|                    |          |
|                    |          |
|                    |          |
|                    |          |
|                    |          |

## DAILY TIME SHEET

| TIME | ACTIVITY | Planned | Interrupt | Priority | INVOLVED WITH | COMMENT |
|------|----------|---------|-----------|----------|---------------|---------|
|      |          |         |           |          |               |         |
|      |          |         |           |          |               |         |
|      |          |         |           |          |               |         |
|      |          |         |           |          |               |         |
|      |          |         |           |          |               |         |
|      |          |         |           |          |               |         |
|      |          |         |           |          |               |         |
|      |          |         |           |          |               |         |
|      |          |         |           |          |               |         |
|      |          |         |           |          |               |         |
|      |          |         |           |          |               |         |
|      |          |         |           |          |               |         |
|      |          |         |           |          |               |         |
|      |          |         |           |          |               |         |
|      |          |         |           |          |               |         |

| TIME WASTERS—CAUSE | SOLUTION |
|--------------------|----------|
|                    |          |
|                    |          |
|                    |          |
|                    |          |
|                    |          |
|                    |          |
|                    |          |
|                    |          |
|                    |          |
|                    |          |
|                    |          |
|                    |          |

# Beware These Time-Robbers

You can't kill time, but you sure can do a number on it.
—DIANA SILCOX

TIME-ROBBERS (time-wasters) are anything that keeps us from achieving our objectives.

Since the purpose of keeping the time log is to pinpoint these robbers, we need a foolproof means of identifying our personal time-wasters, which are not always obvious at first glance. The question I've found to be absolutely vital in determining my own time-robbers is what I call the "Silcox question":

WHAT WILL HAPPEN IF I DON'T GET THIS DONE?

Would you go back and read the question? It's worth it!

If the answer is NOTHING, then that activity is a certified time-waster at that moment.

So if the answer is NOTHING, then *don't do it.*

For example, when I realized I was organizing myself right into an 18-hour workday, I began to ask myself the Silcox question constantly.

*Situation:* Mail piles up on the desk in the morning. What will happen if I don't open this immediately? Answer: Nothing. (In my early days, much of my mail was usually of the junk persuasion and could wait indefinitely.)

*Situation:* Phone calls seem to monopolize my time. What will happen if I don't make those 101 calls or if I cut short the calls that stretch into social chitchat? Answer: Nothing. (Most of these phone calls are busywork.)

*Situation:* A client calls and asks me to come to her office this afternoon, just when I was making some headway into the mail. What will happen if I don't go? Answer: I may lose the client. (I go.)

## DECISIONS BECOME AUTOMATIC

The question makes decision making so much easier that it's become automatic for me. At first, you have to *remember* to ask it when you're debating with yourself on the importance of an activity, but you'll be surprised how quickly it becomes second nature to you, and how easy you'll find it to eliminate unimportant tasks.

Time-robbers obviously differ for each woman. If a secretary asks herself, What will happen if I don't get this done? when she's facing a huge pile of mail, she will, in most cases, answer: "Could lose my job." If the secretary's boss asks herself the same question, about the same job, the answer would most likely be: "Nothing. That's what I have a secretary for."

The important thing to remember is the Silcox question "What will happen if I don't get this done?" and how to apply that question to your own time.

Another helpful hint for ridding yourself of unimportant tasks is a truism established by an Italian sociologist-economist, Pareto's principle, the 20/80 law:

*80 percent of the results comes from 20 percent of the activities.*

For example: If I must answer three letters but only have time to write one, the one I would choose is the one from which I will get the most results. If the choice is among one actual and two prospective clients, I would choose the actual client as the most profitable, since she is already giving me business.

Since results are what you're after, it's superfluous to pursue activities that fall within the 80 percent that *don't* provide results.

Again, you can determine the unprofitable 80 percent by asking the Silcox question; and if the answer is "Nothing," then skip it. It's not worth doing. Most time-wasters appear both at home and at the office; a few specifically apply to the home and others specifically apply to the office. You'll find out.

# A Word About a Dirty Word: "Procrastination"

Delay is the deadliest form of denial.
—PARKINSON'S LAW OF DELAY

LET'S TAKE a close look at procrastination. It'll encourage you to do the time log if you've been putting it off.

Nearly all of us procrastinate at some time. The sick feeling that comes over us when we realize we've procrastinated just a little bit too long is universal.

Why do we procrastinate? Check out which reasons apply to you:

We're afraid to make mistakes, so we just don't do it.

We're afraid of making decisions.

We're afraid of finishing a task, because that might leave us with nothing to do and, heaven forbid, time on our hands.

The task is unpleasant (although, as we'll discuss, we also put off pleasant tasks).

We convince ourselves the task is unimportant. (In some cases, the task may actually *be* unimportant. Learn to tell the difference with the Silcox question.)

We think we have more time than there really is.

The task seems overwhelming; we don't know where to begin—so we don't begin.

## HOW IT BECAME A HABIT

Usually procrastination is a habit we have formed to avoid unpleasant things, and once that pattern has been established it may know no bounds. We'll put off *anything that does not have to be done today*. Like Scarlett O'Hara, we think "tomorrow is another day."

Scarlett, of course, had a point.

But *why* put off till tomorrow what can be done today?

Afraid of making mistakes? The best thing to do is to examine the anxiety and attempt to understand it. Since most mistakes are a result of poor planning or lack of knowledge or appropriate skills, you can make a solid effort to beef up that knowledge or skill through further research.

Suppose you've been putting off a project because you really don't have all the facts you need to complete it. Just *get those facts!* You're probably putting it off because you're afraid of embarrassment or failure if you make a mistake. Do the best you can *in advance* to avoid mistakes. If you know you've done your best, then that's all you can do. Usually it's enough.

Besides, mistakes are permissible if you've done your best. Mistakes are constantly being made—and forgotten once they've been corrected. Do not let the fear of a mistake paralyze you. The more mistakes you make, the more you learn. If you never do anything, you're never going to learn.

Afraid of making decisions? That frequently happens because we just don't know how. It's also because we're afraid to take the responsibility for our decisions. Once we learn how to make decisions, it's easy to accept the responsibility because we're not always second-guessing ourselves and wondering: Did I make the right decision?

The best way to make a decision is to ask yourself Alan Lakein's excellent (almost magic) question:
WHAT IS THE BEST USE OF MY TIME RIGHT NOW?

## NO MORE SELF-DOUBT

If you've carefully set up priorities, the answer should come to you readily. Once you have the answer—whether it's to begin immediately on the project that will get your company a major new client or to spend 15 minutes with your daughter who has just hurt herself roller skating—you'll be able to make the right decision *without self-doubt*.

Follow up Lakein's question with my own and decision making will be easier.

The fear of completing a task may seem a little bit more unusual. It may be on a more subconscious level, but it's just as real an anxiety as the fear of failure.

Free-lance writer Gail Buchalter notices: "When I'm running out of stories to do, I have a fear of finishing up the last one. So I'll wait and then end up having 15 stories at one time come in."

The key to this problem is to remember that simply because you don't have any *activities* pending doesn't mean you can't make good use of your time. Buchalter, for example, can use impending open time to call magazine editors, write proposals, establish new contacts, or even take time off for a few days before those "15 new stories" come rolling in.

"I've noticed that the weeks that I've got two or three deadlines," Buchalter continued, "it gets real easy. I don't have time to procrastinate. I just do it."

*Just do it.* It sounds so glib, but it's the best advice there is to avoid procrastination. And one of the best ways to get yourself to *just do it* is to set your own deadlines. If you think it'll help you stick to them, tell others about them. Setting deadlines helps to alleviate the fear of finishing, since by knowing you must be done at a certain time, you can begin planning for the ensuing time, rather than just having a hazy idea of some unformed time beyond.

Deadlines eliminate the problem of thinking we have more time than there really is. They give us a specific period to work within and do away with that amorphous concept of Time that invites attention and efforts to wander. Parkinson's law is rooted in this phenomenon: Work expands to fill the time available for its completion.

In setting deadlines, we must be realistic. Set deadlines that you think you can meet, not that you think you "should" be able to make. If you constantly set unreasonable deadlines for yourself ("Oh, I should be able to make vice-president in six months" or "Losing ten pounds in one week is easy!"), you're going to be constantly disappointed at not meeting them.

Disappointment breeds disuse. If you get no results, you'll set yourself no more deadlines.

Insurance agent Karen Olson finds it helps her, when she sets a deadine, to tell her daughter Robin about it, especially if the deadline affects Robin. Knowing that she's got two more critical eyes expecting her to meet her deadline is an effective way of getting herself to do it.

If you've confronted your fears and you've set your deadlines and the task still seems too overwhelming or unpleasant to embark on immediately, you'll probably be able to think of any excuse in the world to postpone the inevitable.

*Any excuse in the world*—how familiar does *that* sound? The excuses may range from dusting the ceiling to reading a good book as long as the unpleasant task can be put off for just a little bit longer.

## YOU NEED NO MORE EXCUSES

When deadlines don't seem to do the trick, I rely on the "baby step" method. In fact, I've become so accustomed to doing things by taking baby steps that it works every time.

Stop looking at the offending task in its entirety. Take it step by step. Do it in installments: little ones in the beginning until you see the job progressing. Then you'll have gained the impetus to take bigger, faster-moving steps.

Like many working women, a couple of years ago I found myself getting out of shape from too much sitting. "Exercise," I heard myself mumbling more and more frequently. But "exercise" is such a BIG word! It kept me from getting too serious about getting in shape.

Then I read something about doing exercises in the shower and bath (*Shower Power* by Helen Fleder, published by M. Evans.) *Small* exercises in the coziness of one's own bathroom sounded much more appealing. Finally I started what I'd been dreading for so long.

It wasn't so bad, so I moved into the living room for a few more energetic efforts. Gradually, step by step, my exercise routine evolved into an hour at a spa (convenient to my home) each afternoon. I felt much better physically and mentally, not only because exercise is good for you but because I'd finally accomplished a major goal.

If getting myself to do something beneficial was so difficult, I know it's even more difficult to get started on something that may seem unpleasant or may threaten to add a lot more work to my load. That's why I look at it in pieces. A report for a client, for example, begins with a "baby step" as basic as making an exploratory phone call or putting a blank piece of paper into the typewriter and typing notes to myself.

The *physical* action of phoning or typing usually leads into the next step, which leads into the next . . . But you cannot be afraid to take that first step. Make it as small as it needs to be for you to be able to take it, because without it you'll never get to the end of the task.

Take this book. It would never, never have gotten finished if all I had seen in my mind was the finished item sitting on book-shelves in B. Dalton's or Walden's. Instead, I began by jotting down reasons for doing the book; I asked friends how to go about selling the idea to a publisher; I followed up on their advice and got an agent . . . One step led to the next in such a logical progression that what could have been an overwhelming task actually went fairly smoothly.

A chore half done is worth nothing until it is completed. That's not a proverb yet, but it ought to be.

## CRACKING THE PROCRASTINATION BARRIER

The four main things to remember when tackling procrastination are:

1. Confront and evaluate your fears.
2. Set deadlines with yourself and others.
3. Be decisive, then act on your decision.
4. Use the baby step method.

And, oh yes, remember:
DO IT NOW.

When you stop procrastinating, the payoff is amazing. Look at Rose Gruppuso, co-owner of Gruppuso Plumbing in Yonkers,

New York. She is very active in several professional women's organizations; a single parent, she has raised two sons; she travels frequently on business and for pleasure; she has found time for romance (she was engaged to be married when we talked to her); she also does petit point, needlepoint, crocheting, and painting (both oil and watercolor), reads, has a green thumb and a sun porch full of plants, hunts antiques, finishes furniture . . . and she does it all extremely well.

How? we asked.

"First of all, I'm a no-nonsense person," Gruppuso explained. "I don't dilly-dally when I do things. I guess what I don't do is waste a minute. I don't procrastinate and there's no idleness in me."

# Beating the
# Perfectionism Trap

ARE YOU AFRAID the Snoopy Sniffer is gonna get you? Do you live in fear that your furniture will fail the white-glove test? Do you dread leaving the office not having opened every bit of mail?

If you answered yes to any of these questions, you're a victim not only of the media's presentation of women but also of a major time-robber: perfectionism.

Perfectionism is a sophisticated form of procrastination: If you work at one thing long enough, you can effectively put off several important tasks. And how many times have you avoided completing something by telling yourself it had to be "just perfect"?

Before women began working outside the home, when our primary job was as wife, mother, and housekeeper, we had the *time* to challenge Snoopy Sniffer with the perfection of odorless, spotless homes. We had the *time* to cook elaborate dinners and desserts for our family, to spend "quantity" hours with our children, to pull ourselves together enough to be sexy and understanding when our husbands came home from a hard day at the office.

Perfectionism was a blessing, because we had the *time* to be perfect.

That blessing quickly became a curse when we began entering the job market in force. We, not our husbands or our children—and probably not our employees or employers—are the ones insisting on the perfection we demand of ourselves.

The problem is that this striving is no longer realistic. We no longer have the time because that time has been parceled out to so many demanding users: home, office, children, boss, husband . . . It's still important to do the best we can in each job. What's no longer important is to keep on doing it until we get it perfect.

## YOU'RE NOT EXPECTED TO BE PERFECT

Learn to compromise on perfection without compromising yourself. It's easier than it sounds. Many of us make ridiculous demands on ourselves because we, again, think it's expected of us by others. That's called "other-directed" and it's bad for the ego and unfair to yourself.

I have a friend who spent hours making fresh fruit preserves for her family. At first she really enjoyed it. As she became busier with her career, she continued making the preserves only because she was convinced her children and husband really liked her to do it. But whenever she made the preserves now, she became angry and resentful; she would rather have spent the time doing something else.

Finally she got up enough nerve to ask her family how they'd feel if she quit making the preserves.

"Gee, mom (or honey), we didn't even *know* you were making them; we thought you got 'em at the store."

The point: In most cases, you're the only one making those difficult demands on yourself. (When others do expect perfection, it helps to talk; we'll discuss how later.)

Fortunately, perfectionism is something many working women seem to be coming to grips with .

Genevieve Meek, a free-lance illustrator in Dallas, was raised traditionally: that is, get married, keep house, raise the children . . . A soft-spoken woman who's very close to her husband, Gary, Meek looked up from her dusting one day and realized she didn't have any time to have fun with Gary—and that's what they'd gotten married for in the first place. So she broke with tradition:

"I guess I'm just not as critical, particularly in housekeeping because that's something I don't really care about as much. So I can eliminate some of that time. It doesn't bother me that the baseboards aren't dusted every week and that the windows aren't washed every month. I used to spend a lot of time polishing the furniture, and then being upset that dust would have the *audacity* to come two or three days later. Now, not only do I not have to spend the time dusting, I also don't have to spend the time worrying about it and being frustrated afterwards."

Meek is just one of the thousands of working women who have reached the healthy conclusion that a perfectly kept house is not crucial to a fulfilling life-style.

## DUST ISN'T FATAL

A University of Michigan Survey Research Center study showed that working women spend an average of 26 hours a week on housework; full-time homemakers spend 55 hours. Other studies have shown similar results, but more and more women are deciding that a little dust isn't fatal.

Cheryl Hughes cut down on the time she was spending cleaning house after observing, "Women put such incredible pressures on themselves. I noticed it especially around the holidays when

I was home, this incredible pressure for everything to be perfect. That made me miserable because it was such a futile kind of thing."

She began cutting corners. Now "things are much more relaxed and obviously much more comfortable for all of us because we're not having someone running around the house always wanting everything looking just so or having everything done. I don't hear any complaints. I felt a great deal of pressure to have everything cleaned by 9:00 or 10:00 a.m. Now that I'm working, I could care less. It has assumed such a low priority."

Although housework is one of the most obvious places for saving huge amounts of time by simply avoiding perfectionism, there are unnecessary things on the job, too, that we frequently labor over because we just don't think of "nonperfect" options.

How often have you put off answering a letter that needs only a quick reply because you don't "have the time" to compose a "perfect" reply, dictate it to your secretary, proof the typing, and sign it? Next time something that needs a quickly worded answer comes across your desk, simply jot down your reply on that same piece of paper and return it in the same day's mail.

I've done this for years, and I know lots of others, businessmen and -women who do it. None of us has ever received a complaint of sloppiness or unprofessionalism. A quick reply such as this is much more appreciated than any attempt to conform to textbook standards and perhaps, in the process, delay the response.

## "COMPROMISE" IS NOT A DIRTY WORD

Let compromise replace perfectionism, not only in your vocabulary, but also in your life-style.

Liz Wolff realized she could compromise without sacrificing her own high standards:

"I used to be a workaholic," the Charlotte teacher says; "I'd go to work at 6:30 and come home at 7:30 p.m. I'd do the housework, and all of the things required by my different roles. *Supermom.* But now I don't have *time* to do it. I'm still a perfectionist, I won't say that I'm not; I'm still very conscientious, but I also realize I can compromise on what perfection is and make the best of all that should be done."

The way she does this is to ask herself her own version of my question: "What's the most important job on my list for today that I have to get done?"

It's an all-purpose question, and when you find your tendency for perfection is keeping you from doing something you really should be doing or would really rather be doing, ask yourself:

WHAT WILL HAPPEN IF I DON'T DO THIS TO PERFECTION?

If the answer is NOTHING—then compromise!

# Beating the
# Waiting-Time Bugaboo

Life is one big traffic jam.
—DIANA SILCOX

Time waits for no woman.
—AVA STERN
*Publisher of* Enterprising Women

ONE OF THE BIGGEST time-wasters is *waiting time*. It's also one of the most difficult to eliminate from your own list of robbers, because frequently it's another person's fault that you're doing the waiting.

Difficult, but not impossible. You may still have to wait, but if you plan carefully, *waiting* time will not be synonymous with *wasted* time.

Unfortunately, many people have adapted to being kept waiting by applying the philosophy, "If you can't beat 'em, join 'em."

"I don't like to wait," explains Susan Schein, owner of a public relations firm, after admitting she's always late. "And everybody I know is always late, so I try to be later than them. But that's very inconsiderate."

"I almost always am five to 15 minutes late," says newspaper

84

editor Harriet Simpson. "I know it's because I plan things too close to the line. I think it's partly selfish, too. I really hate to get to a place early and have to spend 15 minutes waiting. I figure that's wasted time. But there are people who have to wait for me."

Joining the chronic latees is, obviously, neither the best nor the only solution.

First, *tell* people that you do not like to be kept waiting. This applies to both people you are *going* to meet and people who are *coming* to meet with you.

Because of our traditional problems with assertiveness it may at first be difficult to, for example, tell your doctor you do not want to spend two hours in his waiting room. (Why do you think the reception area in a doctor's office came to be called *waiting* room?) You may find it just as difficult to tell friends; you'll worry that they'll think you bitchy and compulsive.

The results, however, may change your mind.

Although some doctors are changing their policy of over-booking, they still seem to be the worst offenders when it comes to keeping others waiting. I once waited for two hours past my appointment with my doctor. I was already seething, but then he came out and took a man, whose appointment was *after* mine, into his offices, explaining to me that the male patient was a *businessman*, and his time was more valuable than mine.

Wrong thing to say! I nearly walked out, but instead, when my turn came, I calmly told the doctor that I was a *businesswoman*, that my time was just as valuable as the businessman's. I further explained that not only did he owe me an apology for keeping me waiting as well as for the crack about my time not being so valuable; he *also* owed me money.

And I sent him a bill for my waiting time.

*And* he deducted my charges from his bill!

You see, people can be brought around, and that includes men. Now, whenever my doctor knows he's running late, his receptionist calls me to let me know so I can readjust my own appointment. Had I simply seethed and walked out, the next time would have been no different. I would only have waited and seethed some more.

*Let people know your time is valuable!* If you simply accept waiting, nothing will change and you'll continue to waste time.

## HOW TO WAIT FOR THE DOCTOR

The horror stories about waiting in professionals' offices are endless. Many women actually plan to spend an afternoon at the doctor's for an appointment that should really only require thirty minutes.

Jackie Friss, a training specialist with the New York State Education Department, always makes sure she's on time. But she always prepares for others who'll keep her waiting:

"I took my daughter for a physical, and I decided I would take an hour or two off work. I ended up taking the whole afternoon off. But I also knew there would be that possibility, so when I left I said I'd be back in two hours—and there's the *possibility* I may have to take the whole afternoon off. Which is exactly what happened."

We shouldn't have to adapt to this gross abuse of time. Harriet Simpson, after seething just as I had in her child's doctor's office, walked out after telling the receptionist to reschedule her. That evening, she received a call from the doctor, a woman:

"She apologized. She and her husband are both doctors. Both have a practice. They have three children. I have a feeling she may have been somewhat empathetic to my plight. She said she was very sorry and she had been trying to do something about the system of overbooking for a long time. She added she would

86

be willing to meet me at the office that evening or would take me as her first patient in the morning."

Another triumph, the payoff of *communication*.

## START WITHOUT THEM!

What about the reverse situation: getting people to arrive for your own appointments on time?

When Carol Bellamy was elected president of the New York City Council, one of the first things she did was announce that all council meetings, notorious for beginning late, would from that point on begin *on time*.

The newspapers reported the announcement as if it were a cute little quirk of our new council president. Bellamy refused to budge, however, and the meetings now begin on time, not only saving her own time, but also that of every other person required to attend.

Since, as I've mentioned, time is cumulative, that amounts to several hours of somebody's time.

You don't have to be a city council president to demand punctuality. Rose Gruppuso, president of a professional women's organization, insists on the same respect.

"When a meeting starts at seven," she says, "I start it whether you're there or not. People know what's expected of them, and if you give them the opportunity to be lax and lazy, then they fall into that trap. If you demand of people—and 'demand' is a strong word, but it's the only word that I think really applies—then people feel responsible and live up to those demands."

Calling a meeting at an odd time will encourage people to get there on time. Call a meeting for 6:05 or 5:55 instead of 6:00. When people see an odd time, they know you mean business.

You don't have to come right out and say to your best friend, "I demand that you be on time for lunch." Try letting her know by saying something like, "I really hate to be kept waiting, don't you?" She or he will get the message soon enough, but *only if you attempt to convey it.*

Very few people actually mean to be late. The main reason for lateness is that people simply do not allow enough time for the "little things" that may make them late.

"If anything can go wrong, it will" (or "The bread always falls jelly side down") is a Murphy law truism.

I believe that *"life is one big traffic jam,"* and once you get out of the jam, *"life is one big parking lot that's always full!"*

Prepare for those last-minute problems by building flexibility into your schedule so you'll arrive on time for appointments.

Susan Friedman, doctor's secretary and the mother of an infant, has found a solution that works well for her most of the time:

"I *never* say I'm going to be somewhere at 6:30. I never, never say that. I don't put that kind of pressure on myself, because I do allow for the unexpected. I say I'll be there around 6:30 or 7:00; then I usually make it at 6:30."

Friedman's trick is a good one. Not only does it relieve the pressure on you and allow for the unexpected, but it also clues in the person at the other end to the fact that you may be a little late, which permits the other person to plan her schedule accordingly.

Naturally, the idea isn't always applicable. Some appointments must be much more accurately scheduled, and this is where you must try to allow for those little crises, for the bread falling jelly side down.

Media director Vicki Riker is an on-time person largely because "my mother did instill in me that it's not polite to keep other people waiting, because their time is valuable." She always allows enough time to get someplace on schedule and "if for some reason the unexpected crisis comes up," she punts. Sometimes the punting merely means a phone call to the person waiting for you. It's just common courtesy to let a person know so she can make use of the time.

Planning to leave for an appointment five minutes earlier than you think necessary is usually plenty of time to allow for a late bus, a traffic jam (if you know the traffic is usually horrible at a certain time, plan accordingly), a child spilling cereal, a poor sense of distance . . . And if you get to your destination five minutes early and find you're the one who's waiting, then, as the Girl Scouts admonish, Be Prepared! That, too, takes planning. Here's how.

## CAUGHT IN TRAFFIC

Waiting time is a bugaboo that will always be with us, like death and taxes, though you can make great dents in the *amount* of time you spend waiting, as we've been saying. But waiting time need not be wasted time, if you plan for it.

If I'm caught in my own proverbial traffic jam, I have to know that there's a book in my briefcase that can be read or a file that I can start work on. (I, of course, take taxis since I live in Manhattan. If you're driving yourself, it's not too wise to begin that juicy novel.) Musician/librarian Rosalie Davies uses her driving time to brush up on her singing. Jenita Cargile, a confidential investigator, is learning new languages with the tapes she plays during her Los Angeles commuting time.

When I'm in an office waiting for a client I always have some work that I can be doing; or I'll use the time to catch up on personal correspondence, reading or a quick phone call.

Doctor's secretary Susan Friedman has sensibly come to consider her waiting time *leisure* time and always has a book or magazine with her. The thing to remember is: Whenever you leave your home or office, *prepare for the unexpected.*


## GO AHEAD: DREAM!

Waiting time needn't always be time for overt activity. Just sitting and thinking is a great use of your time for doing some planning. It's also a great way to get started on something you just hate to do and are procrastinating about; thinking can be the first of your "baby steps" toward the completion of the project.

And it's a good time to catch up on daydreaming, also. There's absolutely nothing wrong with daydreaming. Quite the contrary: it's fun and it's an asset.

"Unless you dream," believes Cindy Annchild, co-owner of the Bath House, a shop for bathing supplies in New York, "I don't think anything happens. *Dreaming is a part of my planning.*"

So waiting time can be valuable in a variety of ways. What makes it valuable is *knowing* how you're spending it—working, planning, or relaxing. What can make it wasted time is wondering afterward how you spent it. Rid yourself of wasted waiting time by remembering—and by *doing* these three things:

1. *Tell* people you do not like to be kept waiting.
2. Allow for the unexpected.
3. Prepare for the inevitable wasted time.

Your traffic jam will flow a lot more smoothly.

# *Speak Up to Save Time*

---

ONE OF OUR BIGGEST time-savers is literally at the tip of our tongues: communication.

The ability to communicate well in the office and at home is vital when it comes to eliminating nearly every time-waster. We've already seen how my friend who insisted on making home-made preserves cut out this aggravating chore by *discussing* it with her family. And we've learned how important it is to *tell* people you don't like to be kept waiting. You can't count on people having ESP. You can't divine what's in their heads, and vice versa.

If communication is such an obvious and effective time-saver, what keeps us silent?

A lot of the problem is buried in the traditional female non-assertiveness which we're learning to fight. More insidious, perhaps, is our *assumption* that people around us know what we want without our having to verbalize those wants.

It's hard for us to believe that our husband and children are not aware of everything we're doing and are equally oblivious to the frustrations we're feeling while trying to do and be all things to all people.

But look at it from their point of view for a minute. Just as most of us women were brought up in the traditional rut that we're trying very hard to break from, so were our husbands brought up in the traditional male role. That role taught them to believe that women can do everything! Mom never complained. Men thought she never had anything to complain about. And since she could do it all, they have no reason to believe that you, the woman they chose to marry, can't do it all too.

Men were brought up to believe that women were invincible, no less. Women never got sick; they never said "Can't"; they did everything they were expected to do. Now that women are expected to work as well as keep house, these traditionally brought-up men have no reason to believe that their women can't fill this new role right on top of everything else.

It's more than being inconsiderate or unobservant or even boorish; it's a way of looking at gender roles and it's been ingrained in men since birth.

If *we're* having as difficult a time shucking our traditional image as we obviously are, we can't expect it to be any easier for our male counterparts. But we do. We resent it when the men in our lives don't seem to instinctively comprehend what we want from them. We expect them to have ESP, to be able to x-ray our heads.

The same applies to our children. They may not have been raised the same way our men were, but they still see good old mom as the Superwoman we like them to think we are— unless we begin to let them know honestly that we can't do it all. We need their help.

Cindy Annchild, with Michael NcNulty co-owner of the Bath House and co-parent of son Lincoln, shares everything with Michael—the work at the store, the caring for Lincoln, making plans, and dreaming. Annchild believes:

"There are women who never ask anything of the men they live with, and I think it's as much the fault of the women as it is of the men. You have a responsibility to demand—in a nice way—what you need to function as an individual. It just so happens I need a lot. So we communicate well. Communication skills are great and I think that helps us out a lot. Michael thinks that any problem you have, you can overcome as long as you can communicate about it."

Communication is a skill, which at first may prove difficult if you're unused to talking to people about what *you* expect as opposed to what is expected of you. The skill must be acquired, bizarre as that may sound, and it's not always easy. Here are the essentials.

## NO NEED TO YELL

Good communication is never possible at the top of one's lungs. It's best to communicate before you get to that point.

If, for example, you come home exhausted and angry, *tell* your clamoring children you need a few minutes alone to regroup before coping with your role as Mom. Employment agency owner Margo Berk-Levine spent the first few years of her children's lives and her two businesses *not* telling anybody anything about herself. She totally sublimated her frustrations rather than seem to tread on anyone else's feelings.

When she finally realized that unless she started considering her feelings important, too, she was going to break, she made her first effort at communicating with the family. It worked:

"It was OK to come home and say, 'Listen, I've had a really rotten day today. I need five minutes to change into my jeans and T-shirt. I'll really be OK if you just give me five minutes by myself.' It was funny, I literally meant five or ten minutes to relax, to let the housekeeper stay that extra few minutes so I didn't feel this terrible pressure all the time. It made a difference. I was ready to cope with almost anything, and I looked forward to spending the time with the children.

"They understood that if I was in a bad mood, I wasn't going to take it out on them. They knew where I was coming from. Children really understand that at a very early age. You just say to a child, 'I'm not angry at you, I'm angry at something that happened at the office and I just need a few minutes to get it out of my mind and forget about it.'

"Also, I began to express more openly to my husband why I felt the way I felt, that when he'd see me start to get uptight, that's the time I just needed a couple of minutes. And I understood that he came from a very tense corporate situation and needed his space for just a few minutes too. We each had to work it out so we could help one another and lessen that hostility, that tension."

Berk-Levine's experiences prove that learning communication is anything but impossible.

Obviously, communication can't be a one-way street. "Take out the garbage" may be a familiar litany in your household; you're the one saying it, your husband and children are the ones listening. But unless you sit down and explain to them *why* you need them to take out the garbage and why you would like this to be their continuing responsibility, you're going to find that the job of seeing to it that the garbage gets taken out will remain yours.

Demanding without explaining can sound like nagging.

The magic that good communication can work won't all happen at once. First of all, if you've never made any serious efforts at it, you're going to be rusty and those first tentative efforts may not be very productive.

Don't be discouraged. Continue to explain why you need help, whether it's with specific chores or for your own general well-being. Eventually, your message will get through *and* communication will become a way of life in your family.

Second, if you're not used to communicating, your family will be equally inexperienced at receiving communications from you.

They may not know how to respond at first. They may shrug you off or laugh you off. They may even get angry. But continue (remembering Annchild's words) to "demand in a nice way." Try to get across what you expect from your family and why, and, probably more quickly than you expect, you'll be getting that help and that understanding you need to function more sanely.

While our primary objective is to save you some time, the additional benefits of good communication are great: mutual understanding among you, your husband, and your children makes home that much more enjoyable to come home to.

## MAKE SURE THEY KNOW WHAT YOU WANT

Communication skills are just as important at the office, of course. Although we may think we're more adept at communicating on the job than at home, that often proves not to be so. How many times have you done something and found out later it was not what was wanted? How often has somebody done something for you that was not what you wanted?

Instead of berating yourself or your co-worker for stupidity, think back on the original instructions. How clear were they? Could they have been clearer? Could you (or your employee) have honestly thought you meant something else?

Remember: Words mean different things to different people. If there is any doubt in your mind about either you or the person to whom you're issuing instructions not having a clear understanding of the job, make an extra effort to clarify beforehand, not after the job is done. It sometimes helps to have an employee repeat your instructions. The little extra time you spend prior to the job may save hours or weeks of extra time if the job is done incorrectly.

If the job is done incorrectly anyway, don't hesitate (if you're in the position of superior) to tell your subordinate what the problems are. If you decide to fix the mistakes yourself, that subordinate will continue to have the same misunderstanding, continue to make the same errors, and continue to waste your time.

When you criticize problems with work, stick to the work. For example, if a report misses the point you were seeking, tell the employee what that point was, not that the employee is an imbecile. The first approach is productive; the second generates resentment (need we say?) which can waste a whale of a lot of time.

Lack of communication is just as evident between departments as it is between people. Jackie Friss, the training specialist, has been a victim of such a time-waster:

"I see a lot of wasted time, people duplicating things because of lack of communication. I find that very offensive. If those who're in a position to communicate would let people in on whatever they're doing, it would avoid people duplicating work. Lack of communication steals time from people that could be used to better advantage."

If you're one of those people whose subordinates depend on you to do their communicating for them, then do it. Don't assume everyone knows what's been done. In fact, don't ever assume anything. In Friss's case, she had spent four weeks working on a project which someone down the hall—with a grant and a lot more time—had already done!

In a case like that, it's the superior who should be on top of what's going on in his/her field. Departments are not real estate or boxes on organization charts. They're people, and people can communicate verbally or in writing, though in some offices you'd find that hard to prove.

The key is to be aware of what's happening in your realm of responsibility and communicate it to the people who need to know.

## PUT IT ON PAPER

Often written instructions can be much more effective than the verbal kind. But words are only effective if they're clear. When you write, the key is to keep it simple but explicit (which is what we're trying hard to do in these pages). Using big words or flowery phrases to impress readers can obfuscate the issue. And as we all know, obfuscation can really do a number on everybody's time.

If you'll keep remembering that words may have different meanings for people, you'll be precise when you write instructions. If I say in a memo that I need the report at the end of the day, it would be natural for my co-worker to think I mean 5:00 p.m. If I have a 3:30 meeting outside the office, however, I may be thinking of 3:30 as my end of the day.

When writing instructions and letters, get to the point immediately; it saves your time and that of the reader's. Use the words of common, business language. Reread what you've put down so you can cut and clarify. That sometimes takes two rounds of close attention.

Simple, effective writing habits also prove invaluable to save time at meetings. Write a report with carbon copies for all those in attendance, reporting what was discussed, who was asked to do what, deadlines set, etc. Then, if any misunderstanding has slipped in, it can be corrected before the work begins.

## HOW TO BE LEFT ALONE

One of women's biggest problems in communicating is our lack of assertiveness. Ellie Handsel, owner of an art gallery in Atlanta, finds her biggest time-waster is "people coming in, sitting down, and not realizing I have work to do. I haven't figured out a very nice way yet to say, 'Look, I've got to get to work; would you mind leaving?'"

Do make yourself say, "Look, I'd love to chat, but I've got to get to work or else I'll be in trouble. Would you mind leaving?" There is absolutely nothing offensive about that. Most people will simply get up and leave, not at all offended.

It's difficult at first, but in practice it's difficult *only* the first time. Once you get that kind of a simple sentence out and see that the earth doesn't open up and swallow you, you'll find it easier to do the next time. You'll also find it'll become less necessary, because people will gradually get the message that you're serious about your work; then they won't drop in as frequently to socialize.

Like time, *the effects of communication are cumulative.*

Marie McDonald, who operates her own elevator company in San Francisco, recently expanded her staff:

"When I put the new salesperson on," McDonald relates, "she had to be with me on all appointments. Everywhere I went, I had her with me. I found I was becoming very short-tempered, very irritable. I discovered it was because I had no quiet time, no time to sort out what had happened the previous day or in the previous several hours. I couldn't get ideas filed in my head, or whatever I do with them that clears my head so it's not a mass of jangles.

"I finally said to her, 'You know, we don't have to talk all the time we're driving; it's perfectly OK if there's something you want to work on.' In fact, I found I was bringing work so that as we were driving we were always accomplishing something. That was fine, but when I realized I still didn't have quiet time, I did say to her, 'We don't have to talk, it's perfectly OK to be quiet; I like quiet time and miss not having it.' She then acknowledged she was aware of the same thing happening to her. And that eased the situation a great deal."

So don't be afraid to tell people how you feel. Chances are they see the same problems but are also afraid of bringing them up.

## HOW TO TALK TO THE BOSS

Even if you're the employee rather than the employer, yet consider your boss a fairly empathetic or reasonable person, good communication is vital to a good job.

If you're being given too much work, tell your boss before your inability to complete that work hurts you. Together you may be able to work out alternatives to the work load.

Do the same if you're not being given enough responsibility; if you tell your boss you think you can handle more than you're currently doing, he's going to take greater notice of your skills, not be angry at you for speaking up. If you have a totally irrational boss, be cautious in the matter of communicating. If he's really proved himself to be irrational, it's probably a good idea to look for a new boss.

Communication is another key to effective time management, so if you can't communicate with the person you work with, you may be fighting a losing battle.

Points to remember about communication:

1. Don't assume anything—nobody can read your mind.
2. See yourself from the points of view of those close to you—husband, children, co-workers.
3. Don't nag—give reasons for your expectations and demands.
4. Persist in communicating; giving up means losing out.
5. Make sure your instructions are clear—giving or receiving, in writing or verbally.
6. Explain problems in terms of the work—not the person responsible for the job.
7. Be aware of what's happening in your own realm of responsibility and tell people who need to know.
8. Don't be afraid to tell people what you want.
9. Remember: The effects of communication are cumulative.

# Delegation Protocol

Delegating is the best thing in the world you can do
for yourself.

—VICKI RIKER
*Media director*

LEARNING good delegation skills can save more time than
perhaps any other time-saver we've mentioned.

Delegation is also the skill that most people have most trouble
with for a variety of reasons, not the least being a misunderstanding of what "delegate" means.

Delegation too often means dumping unwanted tasks on somebody else. Naturally, we feel guilty doing this, particularly if
we've been "somebody else" ourselves.

Although delegating does sometimes require some judicious
dumping, a *good* delegator learns to really inspire people by
giving them something to do that will help the employee (or
family member) grow.

Margaret Hennig and Anne Jardim, authors of *The Managerial
Woman*, trace the woman manager's particular inability at delegating to "overspecialization." Women become so engrossed and
competent in one task or in one field that they deny themselves
the chance to acquire the general capability required of an effective manager; that is, literally, someone who can manage
others, not just herself.

Since we are all cast in the role of managers of our personal, business, and social lives, we must overcome this handicap and incorporate basic management skills—planning, organizing, directing, and controlling—into our life.

The mark of a good manager is to train and develop her successor so she can move up the ladder and not be left behind because she's been bogged down by details. The same philosophy applies to the home. Train your family to take over some of your duties and you won't become bogged down.

While delegating may be handled differently at home, than at work, the same general principles apply to both. Let's look at these before going on to specifics of home and office.

## MORE EXCUSES

Although inability to delegate is sometimes a direct result of economic considerations—you can't afford to hire another employee or a housekeeper—too often, economics are an excuse for not relinquishing responsibilities.

Are you using economics as a cop-out? You can test this with the "time is money" formula. For example: "Will hiring another employee free me up to do what's necessary to have our department become more productive?" Or: "Is hiring a housekeeper at $30 a week worth the Saturday it'll give me to spend with my family?"

Once you've established whether money is a legitimate consideration (sometimes we really can't afford to hire a housekeeper or if we can, something else rates a higher priority), you'll be better equipped to begin delegating.

While Hennig and Jardim attribute women's trouble with

delegation to overspecialization, Dr. Sarah Slagle sees the problem differently: "In a household, a woman becomes a generalist, not a specialist. She cooks, sews, cleans, applies band-aids, gardens, etc., so is it any wonder that she moves readily to the typewriter if she types or to the duplicating machine if she knows how to run it?"

It doesn't matter what you call the cause. Women still don't delegate as much as they should, and they're still too much stuck in go-for chores. It might help to think of some of the jobs most of us do probably already delegate without even being aware of it.

Most of us take garments to the dry cleaner's and don't try to remove spots.

Many of us hire lawn services or a young neighborhood helper to mow the lawn.

We pay lawyers to handle our legal work; accountants to handle our books; bankers and insurance agents (indirectly) to handle our money and our policies.

The one thing all these delegates have in common is an *expertise in their field,* and we pay for that expertise. We give them a particular job because we expect them to do the job more effectively than we can do it, our expertise being in something else.

"Delegating," says Laurie Hutzler, president of Legal Management Services, "is one of my favorite things to do. When I sell myself to a general counsel, I'm selling him the fact that I'm an expert in a particular area and that an expert—someone whose business it is to do that one thing—is always going to do that better than someone who's going to do it on the side or for whom it's a low priority or who doesn't really know how to go about it. So I sell the fact that I'm an expert. I know what I'm doing and I've had experience. And I think that you should take your own advice."

## YOU'RE NOT ABDICATING

Ask yourself another all-important question: *If somebody else can do it quicker and better, why am I doing it myself?*

That's basically what delegating is all about: Give some of your jobs to your subordinates, family, or outside resources and you'll find you have much more time for your high-priority choices, work or fun.

The most effective delegation is *not* delegation with abdication; *not* delegation without giving responsibility; and *not* delegation without motivation. And why *do* we try to get out of delegating? Here are the main alibis and the counterstrategies for each:

*"I can do it faster and better myself."*

Stop being a perfectionist. Allow others to learn and make the mistakes you once did. Learn to compromise on what you find acceptable.

Newspaper editor Harriet Simpson finds that delegation is one area she does not have trouble with:

"I think I'm a pretty good delegator. That's something I've *learned* to do. So many times I've felt it's just much easier to do it myself. That's been part of my problem with my children. I overcame these problems in two areas. First, I knew I wanted to go ahead in management. In order to do that, I had to learn how to manage my time and be a better delegator. It was a matter of survival and career development. And secondly, I learned the spirit of compromise. You've got to watch it, though; you can get to be too good a compromiser. But I have to cut out some of my perfectionist standards in learning to be a better delegator, because you just can't be a perfectionist if you're going to tell somebody to do something you could have done better yourself."

Everyone works at a different pace and has different standards.

Although a job you delegate may not be done the same way you would have done it, it may not be a badly done job, just a different job. And sometimes it may even be better than we would have done it.

## WHAT TO DELEGATE

*"I don't know what to delegate."*

Always delegate to subordinates those tasks you know best and can do very fast. Then, when you review them, it'll take you little time. Also it's easier to train someone else when you know the job yourself. Hire real experts to handle projects you have less expertise in. They can do it more quickly, saving you time and money in the long run.

## ARE YOU A GLUTTON FOR OVERWORK?

*"I enjoy doing more than I enjoy delegating to others."*

Remember, practice makes perfect: The more you delegate, the easier you'll find it, particularly as you begin to reap the benefits of delegating: time for more important tasks. If you get too caught up whittling away at lesser errands, the higher priorities will get away from you and you'll get left behind. Life passes by while you're busy scurrying about sweating over mouse work. Men call that "overkill." It isn't worthy of you.

*"What if they do it better than I was doing it?"*

So what? Or better: Great! Give them the credit they deserve. Remember, your mark as a good manager is to train your successor. And if you're a good enough manager to act on this challenge you're not going to lose your job because somebody you delegate to does *part* of that job better.

When we talked to Donna Davis, a sales manager for the Fairmont Hotel in Dallas, she was temporarily without a secretary:

"My secretary was with me for 18 months; we had gone through an extensive training program with her and she got a better job. She's going to be a sales manager at another hotel." It made Davis feel good and look good to her superiors.

One of the major reasons for her secretary's upward mobility was her boss's ability to delegate with two of the major criteria: *responsibility* and *motivation*.

"Delegating gave me a lot more time to get down to the real business of selling," Davis said. "I enjoyed that. I specifically wanted her to have responsibility because I think it's important for people to develop just as I need to develop. She wasn't just a secretary; she was an assistant to me. Yes, she did type and answer the telephone. She also had privileges within the hotel that some of the other secretaries did not have. It was not that they couldn't do what she did. It was because their managers did not delegate responsibility and didn't operate the way I do."

Despite the temporary problems caused by losing such a competent assistant, Davis intends to do the same thing with her new secretary, even knowing that she'll probably leave for better things too.

## WHEN IT COMES BACK WRONG

*"Every time I delegate, it comes back wrong and I wind up doing it myself."*

If this truly happens *every* time, the fault could be yours, not the person to whom you're delegating. Did you train the person properly? Were you clear in your instructions? Did you have the person repeat the instructions to make sure he/she understood what you wanted accomplished?

Loosening up your rigid standards helps also. If people have come to know that you expect something done *your way and only your way,* their performance may be hampered by dread and second-guessing your expectations.

Both these feelings are enough to produce results not only *wrong* from your point of view, but also probably not what the person would have done if left on her own. Don't make all the decisions for your subordinates. Ask the right questions that will lead them to the right answer. Help them to think, but don't do the work for them.

## WHEN IT'S NOT ON TIME

*"It's never done on time."*

Did you give a deadline? Be specific. Don't say "I need it tomorrow." Instead: "I need it at 9:00 a.m." (or 5:00 p.m.) "tomorrow." And just as you should be realistic in setting deadlines for yourself, be realistic with others, taking into consideration their capabilities and other work they may have to do.

If you find you're doing all the compromising and communicating and still have things done wrong or turned in late, perhaps the fault is your delegatee's. Repeated poor performance may require that we replace anyone we have no confidence in, for their sake as well as ours. Sometimes we do make mistakes and should learn from them, not pay for them over and over again.

*"I don't want to think I'm dumping all my work on them."*

Don't *dump* on them and they won't think you are. Do not delegate only junk, but also tasks that will help them learn, grow, and expand their thinking.

Many women compensate for this fear of dumping by doing everything themselves. Musician/librarian Rosalie Davies, otherwise very conscious of time-savers, says:

"Delegating is interesting, because I work with one adult aide and five or six student aides, and I find it's OK to delegate only up to a point. There's a time when I roll up my sleeves, put on my apron, and plunge in, to keep up their morale and to keep them on their toes. I find that's important; it's really important to me that I do some of their tasks along with them. And I resent, and so do a lot of other people, employers who overdelegate."

But Davies admits that when she thinks of "delegating," she thinks of dumping unwanted tasks on someone else.

To overcome this perception of delegation, look at the rewards earned by delegating more than just "the crap." Donna Davis, by giving her secretary responsibility, is able to leave the office, both for business and personal reasons, and *know* that her office will run smoothly. This is a reflection of Davis's management abilities as well as of her secretary's skills. It also gives Davis the peace of mind she needs to handle priority jobs.

Ultimately, delegation saves time; initially, yes, it takes time. Apply the money analogy and consider this initial time a smart investment.

The results are worth the time it takes to plan what should be delegated, the time to train the person, the time to give them the responsibility of handling the job, the time to allow them to make the same mistakes we once made.


## YOU MUST EXPLAIN WHY

Sometimes the resistance to our attempts at delegating comes not from within us but from the people we're attempting to delegate to.

## Delegation Protocol

In a decade devoted to "self," people—men, women, and children—have developed a loathing for doing what others ask. Everybody wants to be top dog. Good delegation skills, therefore, are vital. Orders without explanations, without stressing the importance of the job, tend to be resisted more than delegation done with care.

Do remember when delegating that although we're giving our subordinates or family members the responsibility as well as the duty, the *ultimate accountability and responsibility* rests with us, the manager.

Do not, therefore, delegate with abdication.

A former co-worker of mine was once responsible for a certain project. Whenever I would call to ask the status of an aspect of the project, she invariably responded that she didn't know what was happening with it; Susie Jones was handling that portion. When the project blew up, my co-worker claimed that since Susie Jones had done it incorrectly, Susie should bear the responsibility.

This is delegation with abdication—almost the direct opposite of fear of delegation. Remember: If we've chosen the wrong people, we should admit the mistake and replace them.

If we have selected the right people, we should train them, develop them, let them expand their potential by giving them more and more responsibility—but we should do so with established controls.

Plan *with* them, set schedules and deadlines, monitor their results, and anticipate their problems.

All the women I know who now count delegation among their skills said that it was a skill they had to learn and practice before they could consider it a time-saver.

## THE FEARS AND THE COUNTERMOVES

Teacher Liz Wolff, sums up the fears, the steps, and the rewards that come with delegation:

"I have grown in delegating. It used to be very difficult for me to ask somebody to do something. And then, when I did ask them to do it, to *let* them do it. And third, let them do it and not have me go back and do it over. I recognized that I had a problem and got over not being able to ask people. Then I had to get through the next step (letting them do it); then the next. I'm getting better, but the third step is the hardest for me, not going back to redo the job. It's like seeing a picture that's off center a little bit. It's hard to let go, especially on something that's a high priority.

"I have noticed that once I stand back a little bit after I ask somebody to do a task, I'm observant enough to notice the skills they have that I don't have, and to utilize those skills. Part of that came from a seminar I took; when preparing and studying profiles I would notice how some people would complement what I did—a lot—and that I needed to use that, rather than change them to be like me. I still keep that awareness with me, and notice that some people who work under me don't do it as I would do it, but they have their own way of doing it and I can use that. Even if your way is the 'best way' there's no way they can discover which way works for them if they're not given the opportunity.

"At first," she adds, "delegating didn't save me time because I was still double-checking. But as I've done it more and more and also accepted the consequence of doing it and find myself not thinking about it anymore, it helps save time."

With such great benefits, delegation is too valuable to dismiss. Remember: *It takes courage to delegate.*

## Delegation Protocol

No one can give you the courage, but thinking of the benefits of delegating will make it easier.

Ask yourself, "Am I making the best use of my time—or can someone else do this just as well (or better)?"

A good manager delegates whenever possible. It's good for you and good for your subordinates, at work and at home.

*You must know how to delegate.* And here again is how:

1. Delegate consistently with results expected.
2. Don't delegate upward (i.e., to your boss).
3. Match responsibility with authority.
4. Trust subordinates.
5. Communicate with clarity.
6. Maintain some control.

*You must know what to delegate.* And here again is what:
Always delegate those jobs you know best. When you review them, you can do it easily and quickly.

# *Making Delegation Work at Work*

ONCE WE'VE OVERCOME our own problems with delegation, effective delegation in the office depends entirely on subordinates and our relationship with them.

No question: The secretary is the most important person in the organizational structure. Unfortunately, it's a very unappreciated role.

With today's emphasis on women getting out of traditional roles, we tend to belittle women who remain in such roles. The housewife is the obvious target, but secretaries have also come under fire for their traditional woman's role.

Many women choose secretarial work as a career because they enjoy the duties and responsibilities that go with the terrain—not simply because that's *all* they can do or as a stepping-stone to something *important*, implying that secretarial skills aren't.

My own secretary:

Is sensitive to my time limits and priorities.

Maintains a schedule of my calendar, meetings, projects.

Has regular meetings with me to review projects, activities, commitments, and so forth.

Handles the mail, answers many of the letters herself, drafts suggestions on others.

Keeps interruptions to a minimum by screening visitors and callers.

Organizes many projects and initiates research.

Sits in on staff meetings, noting items that need action, and has a voice on feasibility.

Supersecretary? Not really. Because it is such an unappreciated role, few employers regard their secretaries as having such abilities, so they automatically lose the benefits they would reap if they did recognize their capabilities—and utilize them.

Remember the popular situation comedy "WKRP in Cincinnati" and one of its running jokes, the secretary named Jennifer? Naturally, Jennifer is a beautiful blonde. But Jennifer is also the highest-paid member of WKRP's staff because she earns it: She's the only person at the station capable of keeping things together; she even makes her boss's decisions for him—on the sly, of course.

While Jennifer may be a televised exaggeration, this recognition of the secretary's value is no joke because Jennifer has millions of real-life counterparts.

## A SECRETARY IS NOT A SLAVE

Susan Friedman, a divorced mother of one child, is a secretary for a doctor at a Brooklyn hospital. She realizes the importance of her boss being able to delegate to her and keeps his hectic office running with only occasional input from him.

Does she save her boss time? "Absolutely," she says emphatically. "He does no office work."

In turn, Friedman saves herself some time by availing herself of the "secretary one notch below me." Recognizing the difference between dumping and delegating, she "thrusts off" whatever filing she can't get done to the undersecretary *and* "delegates" the writing of some letters as well as certain case presentations. For the delegated duties, Friedman accepts responsibility and remains aware of what her subordinate is doing.

The result: She has much more time to do the priority items on her employer's schedule.

It does take two to tango, so both the boss and the secretary must be aware of the resources they can either tap in the other or offer to the other.

## WHO DUMPS ON YOU?

One pitfall for a subordinate (secretary or other) is the obvious possibility of being taken advantage of; she must let her boss know if she is being dumped on and her skills are not being utilized to both employee's and employer's advantage. Good planning, priorities, and clear communication really help save time here.

For example, the telephone may be a big time-waster for a secretary who has been asked to type an important report. If employer and employee agree to work as a team on such occasions, they can create a block of time for the secretary to complete the report sans interruptions.

It may involve a trade-off: The boss lets himself/herself be interrupted by the phone during the secretary's uninterrupted block of time. That's a good investment of the boss's time.

Boss and subordinate both need to understand at the outset how much total time is involved; the deadlines; and any other work that may have to be done during the same period.

If you're the subordinate and you think you'll be unable to handle the project for whatever reason—tell your boss before it's too late.

114

If you're the boss, try to understand what else your subordinate may be responsible for, and be realistic in setting deadlines and delegating reponsibilities.

Working as a team really means a new awareness of each other's time commitments and working out a reasonable schedule.

"But," you may point out, "my boss doesn't care, doesn't want to know what my problems are, and wouldn't go along with this plan."

In some cases you may be right. Some people just can't adapt, can't accept procedures that would in the long run pay off for them. If this is true for you, perhaps it's time to reevaluate your environment and maybe look for a new boss.

What may appear as lack of willingness to work with you, however, may merely be an honest unawareness of the situation: how busy you are or how unreasonable the boss's expectations are.

Communicate! Establish the fact that there is a problem and enlist the boss to make plans to solve that problem. Lay out a plan so the two of you can work as a team. Your plan should clearly demonstrate how much more effective you can be in your position if you're able to do certain things, such as accepting additional responsibilities; delaying low-priority tasks; passing on (when possible) other tasks; even eliminating nonessential chores that may still be part of your routine simply out of habit.

Whenever possible, show your employer the profitability of such a plan; benefits in money (especially saving money) get to bosses every time, and this is often a much more attractive way to approach them since saving cash is more tangible than saving time.

All this will take thought and probably some lobbying. But once you've gotten the ball rolling on working as a team with your employer or employee, the benefits will be enormous in time saved and effectiveness of time used.

## IN THE BEGINNING IT WAS TERRIBLE

Media director Vicki Riker, who now believes that delegating "is the best thing in the world you can do for yourself," admits:

"In the beginning, I had a terrible time. I thought, *If I give this to her, maybe she won't do it right; maybe she won't do it at all; maybe I'll be in an awful lot of trouble because she doesn't.* In the very beginning, I was worried about letting go of the reins because I thought my job would be at stake or it would come on my head. But I learned that if you know your people and if you hire the right ones, you don't have that problem."

The benefits for Riker:

"It's freed me up to do a lot of other things that I would prefer to do. It's also given me the knowledge that if I come down with the flu and I'm home in bed, somebody else, even my secretary, can pick up the ball and run with it so the whole department doesn't go crazy."

The benefits for her employees:

"It's given both my secretary and my buyers a feeling of confidence, which is important. Give them some responsibility and let them know that it's real, you're not just making it, it's there. And then they begin to feel that they're getting credit and 'she really trusts me.' It works beautifully."

# Making Delegation
# Work at Home

THE MOST OBVIOUS DISADVANTAGE to delegating at home is, of course, that you can't fire your husband or children even if they do turn in consistently poor performances.

The advantage is that your relationship with them is built on love and mutual understanding, not a paycheck and the threat of termination.

Delegation is just as big a time-saver in the home as in the office. It frees you up to tackle high-priority jobs at work and frees up more "fun" hours at home.

The principles of good delegation remain the same but the application of the skills must obviously be different for family members than for subordinates.

Look at all the jobs you perform at home—launderer, cleaning woman, chauffeur, cook, diswasher . . .

Just as we can assign duties *with* responsibilities at work, so can we at home: a husband can become the dishwasher; a teenager can handle the chauffeuring; young children can learn basic pickup techniques; finances and priorities permitting, a cleaning woman can come in one day a week.

Like the career woman who insists on doing rather than delegating, life at home will pass us by if we continue to do everything without help.

Newspaper editor Harriet Simpson realizes she has a problem delegating to her children, although she has learned to delegate at work. As a result: "I continue to feel that I'm very put upon and I'm the slave and the maid," says Simpson. "My sons do take care of their own rooms pretty well; they do not do much on their own. But they're both fairly responsible, they have paper routes, and it amazes me how responsible they are because I never saw it at home."

## YOU GOTTA ASK

One major reason women don't get help at home: They don't ask for it. Whether out of guilt, hesitancy to relinquish any of their responsibilities, or an assumption that family members should *know* they need help, many women cannot bring themselves to ask their family for help; ultimately, to delegate certain responsibilities commensurate with abilities.

Dr. Doris Moss's theory that many of us believe we are the pivotal person in our household and are reluctant to give up what we're doing—even such tasks as insignificant as doing the laundry—applies here.

We hate to ask for help because we don't like to admit we cannot do it all, and we're afraid of appearing to be failures at our traditional roles after we've taken on the nontraditional one of a career.

Moss believes that other family members are more resilient than we give them credit for, and women who have learned to delegate in the home tend to support this belief. These other family members share the benefits of living in the house, moreover, and *should* have responsibilities.

Edwin Bliss, author of *Getting Things Done: The ABC's of Time Management*, has written that parents who don't delegate household chores are doing a disservice to themselves and their children. That applies also to mothers and wives who don't delegate household chores.

The third barrier to delegating at home—assumption that family should help automatically—can be overcome by clear communication. We must build good communication in the home and not depend on ESP, silent glares, or whatever to get the message across. If you need help, ask for it. If you want that help to be continuing rather than onetime, explain why. Delegating household chores will give you more free time and also turn some chore time into quality time with your family.

## THREE HELPERS

Independent consultant Cheryl Hughes relies on three sources for her at-home help: husband, daughter, and outside.

"I try and get as much done as I possibly can afford. I have a person who comes in to help out with the big housework. We also have recently hired someone who mows and rakes the yard. Shirts go out. We have dinner out on really rough days. We do pay for as much as we possibly can.

"To a limited amount, my daughter (eight years old) helps. When dinner is done, *everybody* works till it's cleaned up. In the evening, we all make a conscious effort to get the garbage out, carry up the laundry; my husband is very helpful with the laundry."

Despite the help, Hughes expresses two of the more common problems with delegating in the home:

"I get help, but it's not a regimented sort of thing and sometimes I get a little frustrated that I'm the one who always has to suggest that maybe this needs to be done."

And . . .

"Sometimes my daughter's help is more trouble than it's worth, but obviously she has to have some responsibilities around the house."

Training children and husbands to do chores correctly will take time initially, just as it does in the office. But it will eventually pay off, and already Hughes sees the benefits of having such help:

"We do have a nice long leisurely dinner and talk things over then and also while we're cleaning up and getting ready; everybody's doing something, polishing shoes or whatever. So that's together time. We really do try to have an atmosphere of pitching in together and that kind of thing; let's all work together and get this yucky job done."

Not every woman is as fortunate as free-lance illustrator Genevieve Meek, whose husband Gary convinced her he should be helping with the housework so they would have that much more time together to have fun.

But some women are lucky enough to have husbands who will willingly help if only they're asked. Once you have asked your mate to help, you should follow the general rules of delegation: Let him do it his way; give him jobs he wants to do and can do well; don't be overly critical—he may be new at this sort of thing and is bound to make mistakes; compliment him on jobs well done.

The same principles apply to children, although something more than good communication may make the job a little easier for them to take. Several of the women we talked to have devised excellent (and surprisingly different) means to get their children to help around the house. Although the ideas differ, the women agree: They have no qualms in asking their children for help; and the saved time is put to much better use. Frequently it's upgraded to quality time with the children.

Following are some of these "delegation" systems. You may find one that you can use as is or adapt to your own family.

Remember: None of these systems has alienated mother and children.

Vicki Riker says, "My two daughters and I always had kind of a camp system. I'd make a list, not that we kept to it totally, and the three of us would split it. But they were in school, and they were working hard too. And I respected that, so we split the chores. It gave them a feeling of confidence."

## RECRUIT THE CHILDREN

Linda Koe says she simply accepted as fact that her children— ages 10 and 11—would help her, and her acceptance translated to the children. In addition:

"My husband and I together devised a point system for them, where they got certain points for the things that they did and the points bought them privileges, like watching television, a special dinner, going to a movie, having a friend over. They're extremely helpful. I haven't washed dishes for three years. They clean up after meals and so forth. On alternate weeks they have dog duty. They now do the lawn mowing; before that I had a teenager who did it. They get paid for that, since it was something I paid the other boy to do. They will help with the laundry; if I have things separated, they can put stuff into the washer and drier. They're responsible for cleaning their own rooms and keeping them picked up. They help in some simple food preparation and take care of lunch and breakfast."

Now that the children are older, they have graduated from points to a budget system, but Koe said the point system effectively got them in the habit of helping her.

Rosalie Davies admits that her three children, ages 10, 14,

and 16, "don't do the housework happily. I *make* them do it. If they don't do it, they get deprived of something. I get a lot of help. The two girls do their chores in the morning. One does the laundry and they take turns doing the dishes and getting each other's lunch. My son carries out the garbage. But then when we have big things, like car washes or washing the windows, I either pay them or I use it as punishment. And I think I'm about to be liberated from the chauffeuring. My daughter's going to get her driver's license soon, so I'll definitely let her do that. That'll relieve me a bit."

## HOW CHILDREN CAN HELP

Liz Wolff also has three children, eight, nine, and ten: "They get an allowance of ten cents a day for their jobs. We have gone through different ways. This year, the children have decided they'd like a monthly job; because it would be easier for them to keep track of them—garbage or laundry—they choose their own chores. Last year we did daily tasks and then it was based on need. I would see the downstairs needed vacuuming or the garbage needed taking out; I'd pick three priority jobs they could do and wrote them down on their weekly calendar. They all make their own beds and do their jobs. It really does help me. Not only the moral support—you don't come home and say, 'Well, I have to do this all by myself'—but knowing they're assuming some of the responsibility and having it helps to get things done.

"When I took my first full-time job I asked for their support. The youngest was five, but they all came through. They all did whatever tasks I asked them to. Since then, they've done it all the time. So they feel good—and I feel good as a parent, because

I'm doing my obligation to teach them responsibility and co-operation and family unity. It really is a benefit to them. I have no problem with that."

## MY DAUGHTER, MY MAID

Jackie Friss: "My daughter (15) is my maid. She hated to pick up her room, and I'd been reading a Parent Effectiveness Training book at the time, so I said to her, 'You really hate to pick up your room, and I really like to pick up. If there's something you'd like to do in return, I'll pick up your room.'" Sue Friss settled on vacuuming, and her mother would do the picking up on Saturdays. Recently, the two moved and schedules changed. To have Saturdays free for more pleasurable things, Friss approached her daughter with another plan:

"I knew she liked pin money to save and spend, and I would be willing to pay her ten dollars a week for her to clean the whole house. I think she enjoys the money; I'm not so sure how she enjoys the actual cleaning. But we have no grumbling and we never talk about it. I don't know what day she does it or whether she splits it up into several days, and I don't really care. The house has been cleaned and it looks OK and we let it ride at that."

Friss's solution contains several classic examples of good time management:

*Time is money:* Ten dollars is a small price to pay for free Saturdays.

*Communication:* Talking intelligently to Sue both aired and solved the housekeeping problems.

*Delegation:* Friss delegated the chore, and lets Sue handle it her own way, giving her the responsibility and trust which makes the chore more than just drudgery.

## PLAY CONSEQUENCES

Rosemary Gaillard: "I'm using a lot of natural and logical consequences with the girls (ages seven and three)—which is to give them choices and help them choose the consequences if they don't follow the choice they've made.

"For example, the oldest had a lot of trouble getting up in the morning. I realized I was sounding like a nag and I was feeling like a nag. I was taking it as my responsibility to get her up, see to it she was dressed and so forth. And I was feeling like she was treating it as my responsibility. I decided I wasn't going to do that anymore. I told her one day, 'OK, Rachel, I'm not willing to feel like this anymore. I go to work and feel just exhausted because it's been so hectic and so hard for me to get you up. So we're going to have to decide what to do about this.' I said we needed to set some rules and asked her to help me. She had some say-so in the standards.

"I laid out the situation: 'You have to be where you're going by 8:00. If we're going to get there by then, we need to be eating breakfast by 7:30. I'm going to wake you up at 7:00. You have to be dressed and ready and have your bed made by 7:30. What should we set as a consequence for the times that you don't live up to your part of the deal?' I helped her see that this was going to be her job, not mine, and that I wanted to help her with it and I wanted her to have some choice about how she did it.

"Together, we talked about consequences and agreed that if she didn't get dressed by 7:30 then when I came home from work in the afternoon, she would have to go to her room for ten minutes. We were going to deny her time with me or she would have to stop whatever she was doing with her friends. Beyond that, my job was to shut up and not nag her, but be prepared to enforce the consequence. It worked beautifully."

## Making Delegation Work at Home

Whether you choose points or punishment, allowance or logic, any of these methods will work for delegating to children, and each one encourages responsibility to grow within the youngster.

The point is: *Delegation at home is vital if we're to have any free time.* Depending on priorities, we may devote that time to work, to family, or strictly to ourselves. But we absolutely must think enough of ourselves and our family to make the effort to delegate work at home.

Eventually you may find yourself in the position of elevator company owner Marie McDonald, whose four children have grown and left home, but who remembers the days when they were still around and all were expected to do chores:

"I don't *do* for my husband and family like a lot of other women do," she explains. "I *share* with them, but I don't do for them. It was kind of a gradual movement from my husband and I being the monitors, to everyone saying, 'Hey, we've got to share household chores and let's sit down and have a house meeting and decide who's going to do what.' I can delegate responsibility real well. You just *do* it. I've never felt that I had to perform around the house to be a woman. And though I didn't have to make beds and dust and clean and cook to be a woman, I felt I had to know how, and I made certain that my children all knew how, including my son. If I was busy working and my children were all home, like during the summer, then I expected them to fix dinner."

# Overcoming Telephone Hang-ups

IF YOU'RE LIKE ME, when you look over your time log you're going to find a disproportionate amount of your day is spent on the telephone, making as well as taking calls.

We've allowed what was intended to be an instrument of convenience to become a major disruption in home and office. Unfortunately, unless we keep the time log, we're probably blissfully unaware of the phone's powers of intrusion.

I often hear people say, "If it weren't for the telephone, I'd get everything done."

Come on! That's like saying, "If it weren't for television, I could do a lot more." We all know that it's not the telephone's fault. The phone is just an inanimate instrument. We must simply learn to control our use of it and our addiction to it.

"Addiction" may seem like a strong word, but if any of these situations sounds familiar, you may be hooked:

You're finally going strong on a major project, concentration unbroken, when the phone rings; you automatically reach for it.

You're just about to leave the house for an important appointment when the phone rings; you rush to pick it up.

You and your family are having a conversation at the dinner table when the phone rings; you excuse your daughter to answer it.

You finally have time to do an important (although unpleasant) project when you spy your phone; the siren's call is irresistible, and you pick it up, postponing that project for just a little while longer . . .

## MAKE IT A TIME-SAVER INSTEAD

Addicted? Sure you are!

Like any addiction, it's a hard habit to break. The good news, however, is that it's not impossible, and once you find yourself free of the phone's tyranny, you're going to find more and more time you thought you never had.

You'll also find that the phone can be a great time-*saver*.

Incoming calls can be handled in several ways.

If you have a secretary, there may be no need to handle each call personally. This should mean more than just having her answer the phone and then turn the caller over to you. If you've given your secretary real responsibility, she may be just as knowledgeable as you in responding to the majority of phone calls.

Newspaper reporters capitalize on this belief that the "secretary knows all" and make a point of cultivating secretaries of important people. Ever wonder who those unidentified sources in newspaper articles were? Many of them are secretaries.

Some people consider themselves too important to speak to a secretary. They don't know what they're missing: a quick, efficient reply, for one thing. A well-trained assistant or secretary can usually defuse the pompous with tact and knowledge and without saying "She's in a meeting," which suggests to Mr. or Ms. Pompous that the boss is busy doing something more important—always an infuriating suggestion.

When a secretary cannot handle the caller, she can at least keep the call from becoming an interruption by answering the phone, taking the message, and passing it along to you for you to answer at a more convenient time.

If you don't have a secretary, an answering service or an answering machine might prove a wise investment to intercept the interruptions the telephone can cause.

## HOW TO USE ANSWERING MACHINES

A word about answering machines: If you're the one making a call and an answering machine answers, don't be coy and not leave a message because you "hate talking to machines." First, it's a fact of life that more and more business people are using machines—if you don't leave a message, you may never reach that person. And second, on an annoyance scale of one to ten, it rates about a ten when the person with the machine gets a message indicator signal—and a hang-up. Beware the wrath of someone with a machine who learns that it's *you* who is not leaving messages!

I know a writer who had been trying to get in touch with an editor for, literally, weeks and was only able to leave messages with a secretary. At the same time, the writer was being plagued by "hang-ups" on his machine. When he finally reached the editor, she gigglingly informed him that she'd been trying to return his calls, but all she got was that machine and she just *couldn't* talk to machines! And this woman was supposed to be a professional person!

Learn to include answering machines in your list of phone courtesies; leave a message (name and phone number will usually suffice).

If you must answer a call yourself and the call comes at an inopportune time, don't be afraid to tell your caller that it's a bad time for you. Often we're afraid of offending someone with the simple statement, "I'm tied up right now; can I call you back later?" Or: "I've got someone with me." Or "I've got a call from the West Coast on my other line." People who do this have found that nobody is ever offended. It often helps to be as specific as possible about the later time when you will respond. Maybe, "Can I call you back in 15 minutes or tomorrow morning?" That way, the caller knows when to expect your call and is not left waiting.

When making your daily to-do list, include a brief description of what is to be discussed during planned phone calls. Frequently a person will call back, and we've forgotten what we wanted to discuss.

## HOW TO END CALLS

When you've taken a call and the business has been completed and still the call drags on (why is it so difficult to be the first to say "I've got to go?"), several effective and inoffensive phrases can end it:

"I really must get back to work . . ."

"I've got to be in a meeting in two minutes . . ."

"Let me just say before we hang up . . ."

"I have another call and really must go . . ."

"It's been good talking to you but I have to get back to work . . ."

Almost always, honesty counts and nobody is hurt. Since it's so difficult to hang up on someone, the other person may actually appreciate your taking the initiative.

Sometimes outgoing phone calls can be just as big a problem as incoming, even though we're technically in control of calls we initiate.

One major solution: *Set aside a block of time for making calls.* Instead of bits-and-piecing yourself to death with a call here and a call there, reserve a specific time for the large part of your phone calls.

Marie McDonald, for example, lives in California and does a lot of business with eastern businesses. She takes advantage of the time difference by getting to her office very early and getting those phone calls out of the way, leaving her the rest of the day to conduct other business.

There are several opportune times to make phone calls, times calculated to get you off the phone quickly:

*Just before lunch hour.* (People are too hungry to talk for too long.)

*Just before five o'clock.* (People are eager to get home.)

*Your own "nonpeak" time:* If you know that much of your morning is a waste for getting real work done, use this time to get phone calls out of the way. If you begin to droop at 4:00 p.m., save your phoning until then. It's much less taxing to talk on the phone than it is to think about important work.

If you're the one placing the call, get to the point quickly. There's no reason for long-winded introductions; people appreciate knowing immediately why you're calling. And it's your responsibility to end the call once business has been completed.

## BEFORE YOU LIFT THE RECEIVER

Before placing a call, have all the materials you need for the conversation handy: letters, reports, financial information. If many items are to be discussed, make a list and know what you want to say before placing the call. These habits will save both parties time that could be wasted "trying to remember."

Rose Gruppuso, co-owner of Gruppuso Plumbing, sums up the problems and solutions for her telephone interruptions very succinctly:

"I get an enormous number of telephone calls, business- and industry-oriented. I discuss what has to be discussed and try not to be too social. Sometimes I'm social, but then it's my own doing. I end phone calls very honestly: 'I'm sorry, but I can't speak anymore, I have a lot of things piled up.' People understand; I've never heard of someone being offended."

Again, when you're the person making a phone call and the person you're attempting to reach is not in, leave a message with the secretary or the service or on the machine, whatever; if given the opportunity to leave the message, always do so. At least you'll get credit for having tried to make the connection.

## HOW TO LEAVE AN EFFECTIVE MESSAGE

Leave your name, phone number where you can be reached, the reason for the call, and at what time it's best for the person to call you back. The last is extremely important, to avoid having answering machine talking to machine or service to service for days.

Leaving a message describing what the call is about, when possible, will alert the caller to get the information you may be requesting. It'll also give that person the option of delegating the call to someone else.

No one's time is being wasted.

## PHONE ABUSE AT HOME

What about phone calls at home? Although our time tends to be a bit more flexible outside the office, and social calls are not nearly as disruptive as at work, the phone can still prove to be one of our biggest time-wasters unless we learn to control it.

All of the tips that apply to the office will work at home. But there are a few additional situations and solutions:

Quality time that you like to spend with your family is too often interrupted by phone calls for you or your children. If you have really planned a block of time to spend with your family and don't want to be distracted by the telephone, *take it off the hook*.

Susan Friedman does this with no hesitation, and has found it quite successful in giving her time alone with her child.

If the call is really important, and the caller hears a busy signal, she'll call back later.

A good time to take the phone off the hook is during dinner, a period that's much more pleasant when neither you nor the children are jumping up to answer the phone.

You'll find your own good times to do this: Saturday mornings, Sunday evenings . . .

Newspaper editor Harriet Simpson despairs of having uninterrupted time for being with her two sons:

"I'd like to arrange it so there'd be a time when you could count on there not being any outside influences: the phone ringing, the doorbell ringing, the homework, the fatigue. If I could plan times when I'd know that nobody was going to come or call, that we could have a beginning and an end . . ."

Taking the phone off the hook is just a beginning to finding that time, but it's an important step in breaking the habit of letting the phone control your time.

## THE JOYS OF PHONING

Like television, the telephone has its good points: It can be used as a remarkable time-saving tool both in the office and at home.

Calling instead of writing a letter enables you to—

- Speak directly with a person, which ensures give-and-take communication.
- Instill goodwill.
- Have questions answered immediately.
- Circumvent the capriciousness of the mail system.
- Forewarn a person of a more comprehensive letter or report to follow; he'll not only look for it, he'll realize its urgency and act upon it more quickly.

To break the *bad* habits and eliminate the wasteful aspects of the telephone, remember:

1. Control the telephone—don't let it control you.
2. Let your secretary, machine or service intercept calls.
3. Don't be afraid to offend a caller with a tactfully worded phrase indicating you don't have time to talk.
4. Establish a block of time for making outgoing calls.
5. Get to the point of your call quickly.
6. End the call quickly and politely once your business is completed.
7. Leave a complete but succinct message with an unavailable person's subordinate, machine, or service.
8. Take the phone off the hook to avoid interruptions at home.
9. Use the phone as a time-saver, not a time-robber.

# How to Tame
# Drop-in Visitors

---

**"GOT A MINUTE?"**

There you are, finally engrossed in that elusive report and there comes that familiar and misleading question. You look up and, sure enough, you see the office Socializer who's got more than a few minutes himself.

Drop-in visitors come in numerous shapes and sizes, mostly regrettable:

Those who have some time of their own to waste.

Those who want you to solve their problems.

Those who really need to talk to you.

Those who are trying to sell you something.

Regardless of category, all interrupters can be dispersed with one simple statement. When they ask "Got a minute?" say "No."

Yes, each type has his own demands and needs, and not all can or should be shut up with an unconditional no. But remember, your time is too valuable to let others, unaware of the value of their own time, steal it.

# THE WORLD'S LONGEST MINUTE

While it may seem simpler to agree to a "minute's" interruption than to appear to hurt anyone's feelings, look at the long-range effects of that interruption.

First, not since the War of 1812 has such an interruption lasted just a minute. Second, even a five- or ten-minute interruption may be enough to derail your concentration, so although the interruption is physically short, its consequences can devastate an hour and maybe the entire workday.

With *chronic* time-wasters, therefore, learn to be firm and say no.

Frequently the problem is compounded by too many people clustered in too little space, a diabolical combination that makes it too easy to waste somebody else's time. One solution: Turn your desk around so it doesn't face the door. If a potential socializer doesn't catch your eye, he'll often pass you by. To interrupt, he must walk into your office and around your desk to speak with you, usually too cumbersome for anyone fishing for just a casual moment or two.

This option can be honed to an even finer point if necessary. Training specialist Jackie Friss works with two other people in a small office:

"I've found that I'm able to give a social nod and just turn away from their chit-chatting by swinging my chair around. And yet I recognize that sometimes some of those people need to have a change, need to get away. Sometimes somebody will have been working for hours and they'll come into the room and stand there and heave a big sigh. I say, 'Oh, you needed a break, huh?' That's all they need, someone to respond, and then they leave. But those who stay and don't seem to take the hint that you're involved, I just swivel the chair."

## THE BODY LANGUAGE SECRET

Friss finds this body language works effectively for her, though she has difficulty verbalizing her wish that someone would leave:

"I think I could increase my interpersonal skills by learning how to say tactfully that I'm working and they're disrupting me. I don't handle people very well if they're far more assertive than I. I stop what I'm doing and resent the fact they've taken me away from my work."

Saying "Go away" is a problem for many of us. Friss is on the right track with her body language solution. Eventually, as she continues to turn her back on unwanted visitors, all but the most bullheaded will get the message. And by continuing to express herself silently, Friss will eventually build up her communication skills to the point where she can tell the most stubborn intruders to go away.

Another absurdly simple strategy: Try closing the door when you don't want to be interrupted. The closed-door signal is universally understood. Or remove any visitors' chairs from your office. You'll be surprised how quickly a stander will curtail his visit.

It's sometimes hard to differentiate between a caller who wants you to solve his problems because of his own inability to make decisions (he finds it easier to interrupt you, even though he may be in the position to make his own decisions) and the type who may really need your input before he can continue with his own work.

Learn to recognize the difference. Media director Vicki Riker, a woman with a wonderful sense of humor, admits that she usually handles telephone interruptions by yelling at the ringing phone.

"But," she adds, "I've never done that with an employee. . . . I've usually forestalled those 'Got a minute?' time-wasters. If an employee comes to my door and wants to just walk in, I'll say 'Ten minutes,' or 'After lunch,' or whatever, so that right from the beginning everybody knows not to walk in without a good reason.

"After I've gotten to know the people, which doesn't take very long, I can recognize the panic-stricken ones; you can tell by their faces. Once they've presented the problem, which usually is very fast, I can evaluate it pretty fast. Maybe within three weeks on the job, people stop *just* walking into my office."

Don't downgrade your interpretations of people's demands. If you have an employee or co-worker whose interruptions can usually wait, tell him to wait without worrying that he's sitting on a nuclear emergency.

Like Riker, learn to recognize those "panic-stricken" looks and others who very obviously need your attention now.

## GET READY FOR DROP-IN TIME

As with the telephone, it helps to set up a specific "drop-in" time. For people with problems that can wait, let it be known that you're available from 11 to noon, or 4 to 5, or all afternoon—the time of course depending on your own job and priorities. But whenever possible, set that certain block aside and stick to it.

If somebody insists that something is vital and must be dealt with outside your time block, and you discover that it's not, let that person know your estimation of his own judgment has just dropped considerably and next time, no matter how important he judges his problem to be, he must wait until the appointed time.

You can be sure his judgment will begin to sharpen up a bit.

Once you've learned to recognize the important drop-ins from those who can wait, make sure they get to the point immediately.

Give them what input they need (maybe a simple decision, maybe getting a report into their hands), but do it quickly so both you and they can get back to work.

The point is: you just can't solve everybody's problems immediately. If something can't wait until drop-in time, try Riker's simple "Check me in ten minutes." Or make a date to see them when you're going to be free.

If your boss is guilty of constant interruptions, try talking to him about the problem. A time log can be a valuable aid. Just show your boss how you can use your time more effectively if, instead of frequent random interruptions, you and he can get together, perhaps at 4:00 p.m., to go over the next day's schedule.

Of course you can't prevent all unexpected changes, but the majority of the interruptions will be cut short.

Once you're interrupted, you must also consider your own priorities to know how to react to the interruption so it won't derail you any more than unavoidable.

Susan Friedman admits: "There are times when I don't handle interruptions well, whether phone interruptions or someone coming into the office, and I get all mixed up and I get involved in the interruption instead of reconnecting with what I was doing before and putting the interruption to one side." At other times she handles interruptions well. That's when she knows her priorities:

"If someone comes into the office and asks me to get something done immediately, rather than taking his word for it I'll make a judgment on whether it really has to be done immediately. If it has to be, I will; if not, it'll be put in a pile with things to get done tomorrow or later in the day."

Perhaps the easiest drop-in to handle is the visitor from outside.

It's much easier to tell most strangers to go away than it is to shoo off a co-worker, employee, or boss. It's also easier to demand that appointments be made. If a salesman just drops in, insist that he make an appointment and come back. Even if you can see him at that moment, it's sometimes better to nip bad habits in the bud. And he's trying to sell to you, so he'll be back—with an appointment.

If you don't have a secretary, you can make an appointment yourself and still save the time that would have been wasted had you agreed to see him at the moment. Otherwise, let your secretary screen out visitors by having them make appointments. She should know your calendar so she can make appointments without disturbing you. Again, set aside certain days or blocks of time to see salespeople or others from outside your office. Just knowing in advance, for example, that Wednesday is your "visitor" day can save you a lot of time because you'll also know that you have the other four days to make additional plans.

## HANDLING UNNEEDED GUESTS AT HOME

What about the unexpected visitor at home? This is rarely a major time-waster, since potential drop-in guests seem to sense that a working woman does not have much time. Furthermore, she's not home during the day, which automatically eliminates a vast amount of time available for the drop-in.

When it is a problem, however, it can be dealt with more easily than in the office situation. First: Never issue the casual invitation, "Drop by sometime." Most people don't take this literally, and will call first if they do feel the desire to come by. But a few people, receiving a blanket invitation like this, will drop by that evening just as you're getting ready to dig into the new novel you finally found time to read.

It's hard to back out at this point; you did issue the invitation. Next time be more specific, like "Let's make a point to set something up," or if you're really serious about it, set the date immediately and write it down in your appointment book (of course you have one for home and office, right?).

## PLAY POSSUM

One way to nip drop-in guests that you don't want to face at the moment is to not answer the door. Even if you know that the visitor knows you're home, don't feel guilty about letting his knock go unanswered if he was uninvited. Home is one of your few retreats from the rest of the world; don't let this sanctuary become a target for drop-in time-wasters.

Dealing with uninvited and invited guests who outstay their welcome is a little more touchy, as we all know. In addition to your own normally diplomatic tactics, you could try taking a deep breath and saying, either honestly or otherwise, "I really have to get to bed" or "I really need to get busy doing my laundry" (or whatever). And if they still won't leave—remember the bull-headed few—you have every right to simply say, "Please leave."

(Since we can't exactly equate children and husbands with these drop-ins, although sometimes they do seem to invade our territory with thoughtless frequency, we'll deal with the specifics of this problem in later sections.)

For dealing with drop-in visitors, remember:

Recognize the time-wasters, the indecisive, the panic-stricken.

Learn to say "No," or "Later," when faced with "Got a minute?"—and don't feel guilty.

Use body language to discourage chit-chat.

Don't take on everybody's problems.

Make a note to yourself on what will be your next step when the interruption is completed.

Set aside definite times for visitors.

Curb your inclination to issue "Drop by anytime" invitations unless you really mean them.

Don't feel guilty about not answering a knock at the door.

Remember: You can't control every minute of your time, so build in flexibility for those unexpected "drop-in" musts.

# Oh No, Not Another Meeting!

Sometimes I feel we've reached the point where the meetings have meetings.

—SUSAN SCHWARTZ
*Department store buyer*

MANY MEETINGS are important, but almost all of us are familiar with those that only waste our time because—

The subject of the meeting does not apply to us in any way.

There is no prepared agenda.

We're asked to make decisions on things we're not prepared for.

We're required to attend meetings held by someone whose only purpose in calling the meeting is to make him feel secure or as though he's doing his job.

If you're on the "required to attend" end of the stick, often there's very little you can do to avoid those unnecessary meetings. Such time falls within those minutes you can't control, so instead of futilely resenting it, accept the fact that you must go— and build the meeting time into your schedule.

There are also meetings that, had you known the agenda beforehand, you might have been able to excuse yourself from.

Susan Schwartz, a buyer for a large department store in Manhattan, echoes many women's feelings with her "meetings have meetings" lament:

"Lots of meetings are time-wasters," she continues; "not all of them, obviously. There are meetings we've been told to attend that don't relate to our jobs or our areas of responsibility. To me, that's wasted time. And that's because we're not always told beforehand what the meeting is about. I wouldn't go (if I knew beforehand)."

You can't exercise the option of avoiding an irrelevant meeting if you don't know in advance whether the meeting will indeed be relevant. If you're secure enough in your position, you could suggest to the caller of a meeting that he prepare an agenda or at least give his employees an idea of what the meeting will cover. But to repeat: Meetings aren't always an option, so plan for those that aren't.

## IF IT'S REALLY NECESSARY

When you're the person in charge of a meeting, you should ask yourself always: "Is this meeting really necessary?"

If so:

Identify the purpose of and objectives for attending the meeting.

Prepare a written agenda and distribute it in advance.

Relate all comments at the session to the agenda and make sure all topics are covered.

Plan time for new details to surface during the meeting.

Frequently, we can cut down meeting time by delegating attending certain meetings to subordinates; perhaps they can learn more from attending the meeting than we can, and then report the results so we can take any action required of us. Minutes taken at a meeting often can serve just as well as being there, especially if you only plan to observe, not participate.

Sometimes, however, a meeting may be more important to you than surface appearance would indicate. Many working women, including myself, make valuable contacts at organizational meetings of professional women. The social aspect of the meetings helps to widen our personal and professional networks.

Before radically eliminating all meeting time, therefore, be sure to think of side benefits of each meeting. A meeting may be discussed adequately in a memo in many cases, but it may be the one time when personal contact is worth far more than the time saved.

I belong to many of these professional women's organizations and, as I mentioned, have made (and continue to make) important contacts and friends through them. I do, however, make sure I'm always on time at the meetings and, for those that I'm in charge of, I insist that the other members know that it will start and end on time.

Karen Olson, who admits to being late to meetings frequently, also confesses to feeling guilty about it, knowing that if she is ten minutes late to a meeting with six other people, she has just wasted a total of one hour of other people's time.

All time is cumulative, including other people's.

I now attend organizational or association meetings only when they enforce strict time limits. Those that always go longer than necessary I either don't attend or leave when I'd planned.


## THE WOMEN'S BUSINESS DINNER

Ava Stern has devised a pleasant alternative to her large staff meetings (there can be many on a magazine or newspaper). If they're detail-oriented, she schedules them first thing in the day, but "if they're large meetings with a lot of people, I usually schedule them after work hours so it can be a dinner meeting. I don't like lunches—they break into my day."

Many women feel strongly about the traditional "businessman's lunch," and it's nice to think that perhaps Stern's "business-woman's dinner" is helping do away with formal, unpleasant meetings.

To avoid wasting time with meetings:

1. Learn to plan for those you can't avoid.
2. Find out if you have an option about attending; if so, exercise that option whenever possible.
3. If you're in charge, determine whether the meeting is really necessary, and if so—prepare yourself and others for it.
4. Evaluate the side benefits of meetings before eliminating all meeting time.
5. Don't keep others waiting.

# Crisis! The Nimble Art of Firefighting

CRISES, the part of life that can really do a number on our time, come in two forms: unavoidable and avoidable. The major crisis or act of God we have no way of foreseeing, therefore no way of preparing for: Your child falls down the stairs and breaks his leg; your company is cutting costs and you lose your job. No amount of planning can prepare you for such disasters, though if you handle minor crises well you'll cope with major ones without panic.

The second (avoidable) type of crisis mushrooms from minor, daily problems that can escalate into big-time time-wasters if ignored or not planned for. Crisis management (firefighting) depends almost entirely on your anticipation of the problems.

When planning your day, always allow time for the unexpected. By scheduling your time too tightly you're guaranteeing trouble and maybe even ulcers.

Remember: Anything that can go wrong, will.

The benefit of loose scheduling is twofold:

1. If everything runs smoothly, you'll have extra time to work on something else or to spend on yourself.
2. If everything does *not* go smoothly, you won't find yourself boxed in by unreasonable plans.

The allowances need not be tremendous. For example, on a rainy day I know cabs vanish, so I leave earlier than usual to reach an appointment on time. If I do find a cab immediately and get to the appointment early, I'll be prepared to spend those extra minutes writing a letter or reading a magazine.

Those of you with children know that almost every morning will bring some sort of minicrisis: "Hey, mom, I can't find my mittens" or "Mommy, I need three dollars for the school field trip that I forgot to tell you about."

These problems only become crises if we refuse to acknowledge that they probably will occur and therefore don't allow an extra few minutes in advance to take care of them.

Anticipate the unexpected; frequently the unexpected can actually be expected—we just don't plan for it.

Next, learn to sort out the real crisis from problems that can wait. Often we're so caught up in things happening that we overreact without stopping to think whether it's of real import or not.

Planning also means setting up backup system for situations that need them. If the baby-sitter gets sick, and you must be at work, you need to have a ready alternative. Be prepared for that situation; it may never happen, but if it does it'll probably be at a rotten time.

Crossing bridges when you come to them is unrealistic. Knowing that there is a second bridge *is* realistic.

Crisis management requires that you:

1. Plan flexibly.
2. Anticipate the unexpected—and the expected.
3. Identify a *real* crisis.
4. Build a second bridge *before* you need it.

# *How to Unclutter Your Life*

---

NEATNESS doesn't necessarily equal effectiveness, but often it can *help* us be more effective. People do exist who can be totally organized amid a vast clutter. Most of us are soothed by orderly appearances. A cluttered desk or a sinkful of dirty dishes may keep us from thinking about what we should. As we spy chaos, we tend to become distracted from our current priority, business or fun.

But an anticlutter obsession can turn neatness into a major time-waster. Cindy Annchild, co-owner of the Bath House, realizes she is a victim of this obsession:

"Before I can sit down and relax," she says, "I feel I must neaten my environment. I cannot relax in a messy environment. I think it's so neurotic because I have only these few seconds to relax and I run around straightening up the house!"

Physical clutter is not the only kind that distracts us. Mental clutter can often give us the feeling that we're being nibbled to death by ducks. The best way to straighten up your mind is to make lists; don't try to remember everything.

Keep a tickler file instead of trying to remember follow-ups.

Keep your calendar up-to-date rather than trying to remember appointments and other engagements.

Simplify your file system for retrieval so you won't have to dredge the depths of your memory for a complicated file code.

Take notes during meetings rather than trying to remember everything that occurred or was said.

Keep an updated Rolodex rather than trying to remember everyone's business, address, and phone number.

We have too much to remember to be able to remember effectively *and* work effectively at the same time.

Again, the benefits of removing clutter, physical and mental, are:

First, we clear our environments of distractions, enabling us to work effectively; second, we save time by doing things immediately rather than putting them off.

For example, by hanging up our clothes immediately on getting undressed, we've eliminated a potential Saturday morning chore of wading through the accumulated pile, *and* we've removed the nagging worry that things are not as they should be.

The messy desk becomes a time-waster when it distracts us from the work we are doing. If I can't concentrate on what I'm doing because my eyes wander to the pile of work on my desk and it reminds me of all I still have to do, I'm not accomplishing anything; I'm wasting time. I'm not working on what is in front of me and I'm not working down the distracting pile.

If messiness proves distracting to you, keep your desk top clear all the time so you don't have to interrupt your current priority to remove the clutter from your sight.

The same thing is true of lists: As you run out of groceries, write down the depleted item on a list; don't wait until shopping day to try to remember everything all at once. Your mind will be free of trivia and you won't forget the cinnamon and have to make an extra trip to the store just when company is expected.

Important: Don't let the elimination of clutter develop into perfectionism or procrastination. Do learn to accept a certain amount of "imperfectionism." While a messy desk may bother you because you can't find things you need, there's no reason dusty baseboards should distract you; they don't affect your work.

Perfectionism and procrastination are real time-killers. If you'll accept the fact that everything will *never* be done, you're halfway to finding elusive free time for you.

Personal organization means you're able to:

1. Rid your life (physically and mentally) of *distracting* clutter, not all clutter.
2. Know why clutter or disorganization bothers you and establish the importance of eliminating it.
3. Eliminate it without falling victim to *perfectionism* and without using it as the means for *procrastination*.

# *What to Do When You've Too Much to Do*

SOMETIMES we try to save time by trying to do too many things at once. Instead of saving time, we become so bogged down by the futility of it all that we actually waste time. The result is the familiar feeling that Ava Stern, publisher of *Enterprising Women,* captures so vividly:

"I'd like more time to do everything better. I'd like to feel more finished, to have more strings tied. I walk around half the time feeling like all my strings are loose, that I'm just never going to get every one of those things finished."

And still almost all of us take on more than we can handle and (more important) more than we really *need* to do. Why?

1. We don't plan properly.
2. We're unrealistic about how long something will take.
3. We have not adequately set priorities or made needed decisions.
4. We're trying to impress someone else or ourselves.
5. We're afraid to say no.
6. We have too demanding a boss (or family).

Each of these problems can be solved by applying one of the principal tenets of time management we've already discussed.

Planning (and being realistic about plans) comes with practice. The to-do list (which we'll discuss in the next section) makes planning tangible. The more tangible a plan, the more realistic we can be: We can *see* what we'll be doing. If we see that we're already committed to all we can *effectively* handle, we must start counting on our priority setting and our ability to make decisions to help us determine what can be eliminated.

Karen Olson says her biggest problem about overcommitting herself is "making decisions on what *not* to do. I think I lose three or four hours every week because I didn't decide *not* to do something. It's not so much the inability to say no; it's just that it's very attractive to do minor things. It's attractive, particularly if you're tired, to do things that are very easy to do even if they could very well wait two weeks. Also I need to feel very good to do things which are a challenge."

If you're having a problem making a decision, remember the Lakein and Silcox questions:

*What is the best use of my time right now?*
*What will happen if I don't get this done?*

With clear priorities we'll find it gets easier and easier to make value decisions on what should or should not be done.

## GETTING RID OF OVERCOMMITMENTS

As for taking on too much because we're trying to impress someone else or ourselves, it's critical to remember that we're not Superwomen and that we *don't have to be* Superwomen.

Musician/librarian Rosalie Davies recalls that "on the job, I think I was definitely overcommitted the first year. I was trying to prove that I was going to be good. I hadn't had a full-time job in quite a few years and was really enthusiastic. Then I started to delete a few things. Last year, I deleted a few more things and this year I'm not going to delete anything more. I think we've got a working situation."

By realizing our very human limitations we can often increase our accomplishments because we're not diffusing our energies to the point of ineffectiveness. We can also cut down on our over-commitments with that not-so-simple no. Remember: Practice makes it easier.

Rosemary Gaillard, who is employed by a family service agency, is aware that "in about every part of my life, I try to do more than I ought to do. But I realize I'm doing that." Her solution has been learning to say no to whatever doesn't interest her or that she does not consider a priority. Saying no to community involvement has given her more time for herself and her children, her two main priorities.

When we are tempted to overcommit to pacify demands made on us by others, the skill of communication can keep us from being swamped by circumstances that we might consider beyond our control.

If your boss is asking a lot of you because he knows you can do the work but does *not* know that it's killing you, arm yourself with your time log and some carefully chosen words and explain why you need help. Sometimes a written report can help support your claims of an understaffed and overworked office situation.

I know a woman who worked for a newspaper where she began handling a job by herself that had previously been divided between two people. Although she could do it, she realized the load was beginning to hurt her effectiveness and finally told her boss. Because her ability to handle the job by herself meant he was able to hire an extra reporter, he was at first reluctant to pay attention.

She persevered, finally offering to *show* him how much work was involved if he would sit in with her on her job for one week. He agreed. As it turned out, the week was one of the worst he spent. He left the office early on the last night exhausted—after giving her a box of candy *and* a promise of additional help.

Before you discard the "talk to your boss" theory as unworkable, try it. You may be pleasantly surprised.

We've already seen that the same type of communication with your family can cut down on your overcommitment at home too.

Overcommitment offers a neat opportunity to brush up on a variety of your time management skills:

1. Good, realistic planning and priority setting.
2. Use the question: What will happen if I don't get this done?
3. Learn to live as a woman, not Superwoman.
4. Practice saying no.
5. Communicate.

# Keep a "To-Do" List

I'm always thinking and it doesn't help to be always thinking unless you keep track of what you're thinking about,
because ideas just evaporate like mist.

—LAURIE HUTZLER
*President, Legal Management Services*

*THE TO-DO LIST is the road map of life.*

That may seem like a rather grandiose way to describe such a
simple act as making lists, a habit that many of us are already
deeply committed to. But don't we often ignore the obvious, the
easy way, in the childlike belief that something can only be effective if it's difficult?

Nobody can afford to ignore the *daily* to-do list as an essential
tool to gaining control of time. The overall benefits are undeniable
and the psychological perks provide additional incentive to
making (and sticking to) the list.

The major purpose of the to-do list is to clear your mind of
clutter and trivia by putting that trivia on paper. Writing down
everything you plan to do for the day, from dropping off the dry
cleaning to writing the conclusion to a six-week proposal, gives
you something visible to focus your time-planning prowess on, at
the same time ordering your mind so you're able to focus better
on each component of your day.

I really believe that nobody can successfully get through a day without that list. First thing in the morning when you get up, you should have a pretty clear idea of what you want to achieve that day or you'll bog down and will most likely not achieve anything of importance.

When you've written down the things or activities you want to accomplish that day, you can organize the items into blocks of time. Presto: you're organizing your time. The trick is:

*Plan time instead of planning work.*

Suppose your to-do list for Thursday looks like this:

1. Get birthday gift for S.J.
2. Drop off dry cleaning.
3. Staff meeting.
4. Begin proposal for client, B & J Corp.
5. Catch up on correspondence.

You're not necessarily going to start with the first thing on your list; you've simply written down the activities as they've occurred to you. Now it's time to assign *time* for each.

Since your staff meeting is probably scheduled for a certain time, let's say 2:00 p.m., we can start planning the day at this immovable point. The dry cleaning can be dropped off on the way to work—if you leave the house five to ten minutes early. Perhaps you can shop for a birthday gift during lunch hour. That leaves the entire morning for beginning the proposal for the client. But consider: Is the morning your peak period? Or are late afternoons better?

If you're more productive in the morning, start the report then. After the staff meeting, when you may be beginning to droop, you can tackle that correspondence; it doesn't require as sharp a mind as the report. If your peak periods run opposite to this schedule, readjust your time allotments: Open and answer the mail in the morning and begin the report after lunch or after the staff meeting.

## THE HIDDEN PAYOFFS

Just because the to-do list looks fairly simple, and the day ahead may look optimistically clear, doesn't mean we're not aware that any number of crises might break in at any time.

But by writing down what you want to accomplish, by not building your schedule so tightly that any *one* crisis (not planned) will ruin your day, you can make the best use of your time. And, as we've mentioned, if the day is free of the normal interruptions, you've earned that much more time to either do more work on a report or catch up on more C priorities, which we'll talk about in the next section.

My basic belief is that each day is worth living only if you have a goal or objective, even if that goal is to go to the movies all day. Everybody should set at least one goal every single day and then move to attain that. The to-do list is a guide to help you follow the plan of action to attain that goal.

Trying to commit the list to memory is ridiculous. What for? There may be a lot of items and there always are crises, always interruptions. You may lose sight of your priorities as interruptions take precedence. But if you've written your priorities down, you'll be able to look at the list, refocus, remind yourself you had something else planned, and ask yourself:

*"Is this interruption really more important than what I was planning to do?"*

Even when the interruption takes precedence, the list is an excellent reminder of what you must go back to following the interruption.

## HYSTERIA!

Everybody who makes lists has different systems. Just as we sometimes feel that the meetings are having meetings, so on some days we feel that we should have a master list to index all our lists.

Listmaking can sometimes defeat the purpose of organizing time. Cindy Annchild (co-owner of the Bath House), who loves organization and jokes that she has a file clerk's mind, still has a problem with lists:

"My personal style is *la grande* hysteria. But within that, there is a system. I don't like to carry a purse or briefcase; I like to travel free. But the price I pay for that is sometimes confusion because I have a calendar at home and one at the store, and I have to keep in mind what I have at the store when I'm at home looking at my calendar because the two never meet on my person. I was trying to balance all these things in my mind and I was getting crazy, so I sat down and took a piece of paper and put down THURSDAY and wrote what I had to do Thursday, then Friday—through Sunday. This broke it down for me; rather than this huge mass of appointments and things I needed to get done, it became "to-do Thursday" and "to-do Friday." Now here we are on Thursday, and it's going OK—or is it Friday?"

Annchild waits until things are really confusing before she begins her lists, not because she hates lists, but because she thrives on them:

"I have a tendency to be a listmaker par excellence and I spend more time making them than getting down to work."

Again, the best way to make lists is the easiest way: Keep them simple and pare all your lists down to one list.

I keep my datebook with me, and I write everything down—all my expenses, my appointments, my phone calls, my personal errands—everything is written in that one book that's with me at all times.

## ALL IN ONE PLACE

Marie McDonald, who operates her own elevator company, has a system that is very similar:

"I have a calendar book, one of the large 8-½ by 11's, and I use that for *everything*. I enter in that everything I need to do, including doctor's appointments, people's birthdays, expenses, and plans for weekends. And I carry that around with me. I'm known for my briefcase; I never go anywhere without it. And that helps because I don't have slips of paper or several different sources to consult. I try to accomplish by the end of the week what's on that week's agenda. Many times I don't, and there's a holdover. When there is a holdover I just write down 'follow-up' on a piece of paper and clip it into the next week, and try to catch up on it."

The advantage of having everything in one place like a calendar is that we can keep a running to-do list in immediate conjunction with our daily lists and can carry things forward when necessary so they won't be forgotten.

An important side benefit is the habit of recording expenses day to day. It saves a great deal of time come income-tax season because everything is all together.

## ALL IN TWO PLACES

Commercial banking representative Linda Koe, on the other hand, with a husband and two children in addition to her job, finds it easier to keep two lists:

"I try to do the office list the first thing when I get to work. I keep a to-do file. The list, on a sheet of yellow paper, is clipped to the front of the file, and inside are any little notes and papers related to the immediate to-do. And I have a weekly calendar where I kept all my *personal* appointments and social and family things—going to the cleaner and that sort of thing. Each day I make out a three-by-five card of things that I need to do related to my family and home."

Koe keeps her personal and office lists separate, and finds the system works well for her.

## MORE BENEFITS

The benefit of the simplified list system is obvious:

"Listmaking has organized a million pieces of paper that I usually stuffed in pockets or purses," says Judy Sommerschield, owner of Schield Personnel. "I'm very much of a list person." Sommerschield, who juggles two offices as well as several roles— career, wife, mother, self—also separates her personal and professional lists.

The main danger in this two-list system is the same problem Annchild has: When the lists never meet, conflicts may pop up. Still, if you keep both lists simple, you can carry both with you and avoid conflict.

Many women make lists only on days when they know they have a lot to do. Although this is fairly logical, the advantage to making a daily to-do list, regardless of the busyness of the day, is that it gets you in the habit of planning your time. The more regularly you evaluate and plan your time, the more expert you'll become at it and the more control you'll have over it.

If you only plan the busy days, it tends to become crisis management and lacks an overall plan for continuity.

Although most women do make lists in some form or another and those who do regard these to-do lists as essential in keeping them on track, some women cannot bring themselves to make lists, although they too are aware of how helpful the lists can be:

"I try to find alternatives to 'to-do lists,'" says Karen Olson. "I have a psychological block against a piece of paper with a list of things to do. I have experimented with different alternatives that don't look like lists. I tried putting files on top of my desk with A, B, and C on them, and putting pieces of paper in these. That's kind of ungainly, and there's a tendency to handle pieces of paper more than once. The files end up getting buried under a bunch of things that have flown in on top of them and not been put away, so that doesn't work. Now I'm just about back to attempting to force myself to write lists again."

## OVERCOMING A BLOCK

If you also have a psychological block against lists, one way to overcome such a block is to apply the "baby step" method of tackling what seems like an overwhelming or unpleasant job. The first day, write down one thing you want to accomplish, no matter how small:

1. Walk the dog.

Each day after that, add one item or more. You'll probably notice quickly that your mind is a little clearer. More gradually, you should notice that you're accomplishing more than you did prior to making the lists.

Listmaking yields two definite psychological benefits:

First, writing things down, rather than relying on mental lists, gives the activity a more "authoritative" appearance. We become more committed to something we've put in writing, even though we may be the only ones to see it. The written-down activity takes on urgency just because it doesn't float somewhere in our own mental ambiguity.

Free-lance illustrator Genevieve Meek, for example, only makes lists "if it's the kind of day where a lot of little things have to be taken care of. I usually list items in order of their priorities and try to make it to the bottom." She needs lists on these busy days "because I usually feel like I've got authority in writing things down . . . I just figure if I'm planning, I'd stick pretty much to the plan."

Since that's the whole idea behind the to-do list—sticking to your plans—that list gives you the psychological impetus to accomplish what you've written down.

The second psychological perk is the satisfaction of crossing things off the written list when you've accomplished them.

One woman makes lists for this reason alone. She believes she could probably remember everything she has to do each day, but she loves to see how much she's accomplished. Each morning she makes her list and each evening she crosses off each item that she's completed, giving herself a little "I feel good about the day" boost as she does it.

## BEST TIMES FOR LISTMAKING

Just as nearly anything that becomes part of your daily routine becomes easy, so does making your to-do list. Incorporating it into your day can become even easier if you select a certain time each day. Either first thing in the morning or last thing at night is best. That way, when you start your day you've started with a plan.

Either as the last thing I do before I leave my office or on the bus or cab ride home, I think about what I have to do the next day. That's when *I* start preparing my to-do list. Other people do it in the morning over their coffee perhaps.

There is no right or wrong time. I do suggest picking a specific time each day just because whatever becomes habit becomes easier.

The five or ten minutes you spend on your list may literally save hours each day.

Victor Hugo once said, "He who every morning plans the transaction of the day and follows out that plan, carries a thread that will guide him through the maze of the most busy life. But where no plan is laid, where the disposal of time is surrendered merely to the chance of incidence, chaos will soon reign."

Remember:

1. The to-do list is the road map of your life. Make the to-do list part of your daily routine.
2. The to-do list transfers the clutter of your mind to paper.
3. Organize your time, not things.
4. Don't plan for every minute of your day; leave spaces for the "unexpected."
5. Don't overdo the to-do list; that could reduce, not increase your effectiveness.
6. Choose a system that's right for you—but keep it simple.
7. Keep your to-do list with you at all times—and refer to it often.
8. Use the to-do list as a work schedule:
   - First enter all deadline matters—reports, meetings, presentations, plans—everything that *must* be completed today.
   - Next enter important activities or projects that need to be completed as soon as possible.

- Next enter activities or projects that are of lesser importance with no specific deadline.
- And next, enter activities or projects that can be started today.
- Last, number all the projects or activities in order of importance so that all deadline material will be finished first before going on to activities that don't have an immediate deadline. (See sample lists on following pages.)

# DAILY "TO-DO" LIST

Date __4/5/79__

Objectives: (1) _Enroll in bus. course_  Complete XYZ report
(3) _Marketing plan (staff mtg.)_  Finalize plan for weekend

| TIME | PROJECT/ACTION | PRIORITY | DEADLINE | COMMENTS° |
|------|----------------|----------|----------|-----------|
| 8:15 – 8:30 a.m. | Discuss plan for weekend w/ family | A-4 | | |
| 9:00 – 10:30 a.m. | XYZ project - complete | (A-1) | 4/7/79 | |
| | Reschedule S. King's appointment for 4/18/79 | B-2 | | ask Sally to reschedule |
| 11:30 – Noon a.m. | Call school - Re course | A-2 | | When is enrollment deadline? |
| | Call Harris - discuss his suggestions | B-3 | | Suggestions good - tell him |
| Noon – 1 p.m. | Lunch mtg. w M. Jones | B-1 | | Discuss Baker study bring report along |
| 1:30 – 2:00 p.m. | Prepare for 2 o'clock mtg. | | | Prepare agenda |
| 2:00 – 2:45 p.m. | Staff mtg. · discuss marketing plan | A-3 | | Ask staff for suggestions |
| 3:00 – 5:00 p.m. | Answer correspondence | C-1 | | |
| | Start report - - prepare outline | C-2 | 4/15/79 | Need files before starting |
| on way home | Pick up cleaning | C-3 | | |
| | Go to drugstore | C-3 | | |

°This space can be used for further description of action items and comments, i.e., "Delegate to secretary"; "Don't accept responsibility in future." "Consolidate with other jobs."

# DAILY "TO-DO" LIST

Date _____

Objectives:  (1) _____  (2) _____
             (3) _____  (4) _____

| TIME | PROJECT/ACTION | PRIORITY | DEADLINE | COMMENTS° |
|------|----------------|----------|----------|-----------|
|      |                |          |          |           |
|      |                |          |          |           |
|      |                |          |          |           |
|      |                |          |          |           |
|      |                |          |          |           |
|      |                |          |          |           |
|      |                |          |          |           |
|      |                |          |          |           |
|      |                |          |          |           |
|      |                |          |          |           |
|      |                |          |          |           |
|      |                |          |          |           |
|      |                |          |          |           |
|      |                |          |          |           |
|      |                |          |          |           |
|      |                |          |          |           |
|      |                |          |          |           |
|      |                |          |          |           |
|      |                |          |          |           |
|      |                |          |          |           |
|      |                |          |          |           |
|      |                |          |          |           |
|      |                |          |          |           |
|      |                |          |          |           |

° This space can be used for further description of action items
and comments, i.e., "Delegate to secretary"; "Don't accept
responsibility in future." "Consolidate with other jobs."

# How to Establish Priorities

---

Each segment of my life has another priority: I have
priorities at work and priorities with the children and
priorities in my own life. Keeping all the priorities straight
is a constant battle.

—LIZ WOLFF
*Teacher*

IT SOUNDS SO EASY: Establish your priorities, and stick to
them.

But how do you decide what's most crucial among crucials?
Raising the children right is *crucial* to their health and welfare.
Performing well at work is *crucial* to keeping your job. Taking a
four-day weekend alone is *crucial* to your health and welfare.

So what comes first when?

There's no universal answer to this problem of unraveling conflicting priorities. Part of it lies in the life values you've established for yourself. Sometimes it's a matter of crisis management
and becomes obvious: You're working on a top-priority assign-
ment for your job and the phone rings; it's your baby-sitter
informing you one of your children has taken ill. No decision-
making problems there.

So setting priorities is not a one-time, inflexible ranking.

Realistically, priorities are constantly shifting. Sometimes they even change from moment to moment. As you get one priority done, another takes its place. As a new idea develops, it may replace something that you thought was most important earlier. As a crisis breaks it very well may override what you're working on at the moment. The key is: Don't lose sight of your priorities (note the plural!) within all this shifting. As each new event takes place, it's time to reevaluate your priorities.

If all this shifting and changing goes on daily, why bother to set priorities to begin with?

If you're like myself, and I am sure you are, it works like this: As I sit down and develop my goals, I can think of hundreds of things I want to accomplish. Each evening when I plan my activities for the next day, the list goes on and on and on. How can one person do it all? Superwoman couldn't. Nobody can accomplish what I set for myself. And yet people continually comment on how much I accomplish. And I do accomplish a good deal. The secret: I don't do everything I *thought* needed to be done, because it really didn't need to be done *today*. But I did do everything that was important. And that is why setting priorities becomes such an important aspect of good time management. It flushes out what's most valuable to you. It sorts "the big ones" from "the little ones."

As with anything else, the best way to establish your priorities is to take time out from the doing of things and evaluate what it is you really want to be accomplishing *now, today*.

## GETTING THEM STRAIGHT

When I first began writing down my priorities, I tried several ways of keeping them straight: listing them in order, with top priority becoming number one on the list and the least important last; or only listing the top-priority items.

I kept returning to the system I learned from Alan Lakein because I found it the most effective and the easiest: the ABC Priority System. With the other methods I had no way of seeing at a glance how important number four on my list really was. Was it really a high-priority activity or was it something that would be nice if I could get it done today, but nothing drastic would happen if I didn't? Since I had not set any cutoff point separating the really important from the optional, how could I tell what I'd truly like to get accomplished and what could wait until later, if necessary?

Setting priorities is a *must* whenever we have more than one thing to do—and everybody, of course, does: goals we hope to achieve, activities we plan to accomplish. Without priorities you're scurrying around in an impenetrable maze like the proverbial chicken without a head.

## EN ROUTE TO THE PROMISED LAND

I'll discuss the overall life values later, but we must keep in the back of our minds that many of our daily priority activities had best be based on whatever we determine our most important life values to be. If our most important priority goal at home is to improve the relationship with our family, a priority activity may be to take the phone off the hook during dinner so we can spend that hour alone with the family. At work, a priority *goal* may be to develop a plan for our career advancement. A priority *activity* for that goal may be to check with local colleges about courses in business administration. The point: "Trivia" aren't always trivial. They can be a bridge to the promised land.

Naturally, you won't want to write down on your daily list: "Improve Relationship with Family" or "Career Advancement," and accomplish these grand tasks in one day. It's unrealistic and intimidating to the point where you might be put off from doing anything at all toward achieving such far-off goals.

Thus the right to-do list is a list of steps toward those goals, not a list of the ultimate goals themselves. By breaking down your days, this way, you can set priorities logically and eventually move to new priorities, always progressing toward your grand design: your goals.

## OOPS, IT'S NOT GOING AS PLANNED

During the course of the day, new events may drastically alter your original plan of daily priorities, which is why a flexible plan is so important. You're working away on a presentation that's due next week when your boss comes in and says the auditors are coming tomorrow and everything has to be ready for them. For the moment the presentation becomes a lower priority. The items on the bottom of your list may not get done today because of the new activity. That's all right. If they really belong on the bottom, they probably don't need to be done today anyway. As soon as you have completed getting the information for the auditors you'll go back to the presentation, and then on to the next priority, and so on.

The system is as basic as ABC. So take your to-do list and follow Lakein's ABC Priority System:

"Write a capital A to the left of items on the list that have a high value; a B for those with medium value; a C for those with low value. As you do this, you know that to some extent you're guessing. You're not sure you'll hit the value exactly. That's OK, too. Comparing the items with one another will help you come up with reasonable ABC priority choices for every entry on the list as of that moment. It's not hard. The juggling is even fun!

"You get the most out of your time by doing the A's first and saving the B's and C's for later. Taking account of the time of day and the urgency of the times, you can break them down further so that A items become A-1, A-2, A-3, and A-4."*

You'll also have B-1's and C-4's on your list. But the A items are what you should concentrate on; they are your priority items *right now.*

Sometimes you may have difficulty making up your mind about your priorities of the moment. Lakein's question is invaluable here:

*What is the best use of my time right now?*

Learn to turn this question into an automatic thought process, a reflex. Then setting priorities and knocking off items throughout the day will become practically as reflexive.

The advantage to writing down the A-to-C classifications on your list is that you'll always have the list with you and can refer to it when your day seems to be getting out of hand. Instead of having to delve into a mental clutter that's being overloaded with conflicting demands, you'll have a neatly organized list, a road map that spells out everything, making it that much easier to regroup your priorities.


## LIVING WITH YOUR ABC'S

Commercial banking representative Linda Koe has incorporated the ABC system into her life and feels she has control over her time—most of the time.

* *How to Get Control of Your Time and Your Life* by Alan Lakein (Peter H. Wyden, 1973).

"I am not *always* in control of my time. I think I'm not in control when I get into an overload situation. I plan my time, whether it's something at home or whatever, and all of a sudden something comes riding in out of the blue. I can usually adjust unless many things start coming all at once. That can be frustrating, and at that point I think I'm out of control. When I feel myself getting that way, if I can just step back and see myself, be the spectator rather than the participant, usually I can sort things out a lot better and get back on the track by saying 'No, this isn't my A—it'll have to wait.' Planning has become my lifestyle. And when things start happening very quickly, either at work or home, if I can just wait a minute—*and it'll just take 60 seconds*—and think rather than react to the environment, but say 'OK, this has got to be an A,' and so forth, I find that life goes fine."

Teacher Liz Wolff is also extremely conscious of the importance of setting priorities and constantly reordering them:

"I have many different roles and I find, depending on where I am, that one role becomes more important than another. It requires flexibility. And I have to adjust. Right now, for example, my job is new, so I'm going to put a lot of my energy into that. For the past five years I've been continually reassessing where I want to go. Establishing priorities means I'm not floundering. It makes it easier for me to look at my life and weigh it. It's a very positive process, not something I just fall into, and at the same time I can be receptive to ideas that I had not thought of before.

"Usually in the morning I'll make a list of three or four absolute musts, which I'll carry with me all day. Whenever I leave one role, I make an analysis of what I need to do next time I'm in that role."

Wolff devised her listmaking and priority-setting system on her own. She made it easier to set her priorities, despite her many conflicting roles, by asking her own question:

*What's the most important job for the day that I have to get off my list?*

Remarkably similar to Lakein's and my own questions, it has helped her constantly to determine what she should be doing at any given time because—and she echoes the sentiments of all of us—

"There's just not enough time to do everything that you want to do, and you just have to pick what it is you want to do."

Dr. Doris Moss offers another view of setting priorities: "Copping out is OK. And that's very hard for us to handle. *It's OK to cop out*—if it's for something that's productive and important and is going to somehow make you feel better and as a result make everyone around you feel better."

In other words, by tagging one or two items as priorities, we're making other things less important, *copping out* of doing them. Do remember that copping out is OK. It's for a good cause. We can't possibly have a list made wholly of A-1's; we'd go crazy trying to be the Superwoman who'd even try to carry out such a list.

Remember, too, that your priorities are just that—*your* priorities. Everyone's priorities differ, just as they constantly change. Because yours are different from Ms. Jones's does not make them less important.


Whether your priorities are your family, your job, yourself, or your neighborhood, do work within your priorities when you plan your daily time. Then the to-do list breaks those priorities down into the doable tasks and the ABC system ranks the importance of those tasks at a glance.

When establishing priorities:


1. Never lose track of your long-term goals, even while doing the smallest jobs.

2. Always establish A, B, and C priorities, then follow through in order of importance.
3. Do first things first.
4. If stymied, ask yourself, "What is the best use of my time right now?" and "What will happen if I don't do it?"
5. Do not belittle the importance of your priorities.

# Flexibility: The Liberating Art of Loosening Up

> Life is what happens while you're busy making plans.
> —ROSEMARY GAILLARD
> *Family service agency worker*

> Plans are only a direction, but no one says you have to stay on that road. Take a side road if you want to.
> —ROSE GRUPPUSO
> *Co-owner, Gruppuso Plumbing*

WHILE WOMEN are natural-born planners, I have found that many nevertheless resist the idea of planning their personal time at home, time for being with the family and for themselves.

Primarily they worry that too much *rigid* planning will preclude spontaneity in life; that fun will be planned right out of existence.

Since we do have to plan the majority of our time whether we like it or not—office hours, children's bedtime, PTA meetings, and other *musts*—we naturally like to keep extra hours open for unexpected pleasures: a picnic with the family, an invitation to dinner from a male friend, an hour soaking in a bubble bath . . .

The trouble is simple: Too many people equate planning with rigidity. This is a misunderstanding, sometimes even a psychological block, that you must overcome if you're going to gain control of your time.

*Planning means more spontaneity, not less, in your life.*

Alan Lakein, for example, does not own a television set. When he wants to watch a show, he'll check himself and his family into a motel with a TV. To me that's a beautiful case of rigidity. And that's where I differ from most of the other time management experts:

I want my life to be very flexible: I want plenty of spontaneity in there! I don't want everything to be so tightly planned that every second of my day is scheduled so that if something new and exciting enters my life, I can't respond to it.

## WHEN THE TIME EXPERT IS WRONG

Not having a television is telling yourself that you can't control your time, that television controls you. I love to watch quiz shows. Many people would consider this an appalling waste of time. So what? I'm entitled to my tastes, right?

But when I'm doing something pretty mindless, I want to know very consciously that I made that decision to watch those shows for whatever it's worth—and accept it. So if I'm watching "$20,000 Pyramid," I'm doing it because that's what I need in my life at this moment—something to goof off, to relax and completely separate me from everything else that happened during the day.

*To me, that's the best use of my time at that moment, and I know it and act on it!*

Spontaneity is more than just the right to choose "time-wasting" activities: it's the ability to admit unscheduled activities into your plans without losing sight of your main priorities and without guilt.

## HOW TO PLAN FOR FLEXIBILITY

Betty Harragan, author of *Games Mother Never Taught You* and the parent of one daughter, does not believe in excessive planning either: "You have to be flexible in general. The rigidity of tightly scheduled planning is often the worst enemy in the long run."

So do plan with built-in flexibility. Do not plan every minute of your days at work or at home. It may look fabulous on paper, but it will only prove disastrous in practice. It'll fall apart and frustrate and maybe depress you.

Two extremely active women, who are also two of the most careful planners we talked to in preparing this book, lead very spontaneous lives. Rose Gruppuso disagrees with the belief that planning stifles spontaneity:

"I'm an extremely spontaneous person. Even though I do plan many things, I don't let planning put me in a prison. I'm extremely flexible so I can change my plans. Plans are only a direction; no one says you have to stay on that road. Take a side road if you want. Planning *gives* me flexibility. It doesn't give me rigidity, and it doesn't stifle me at all. What it does is give me more time to do more things that I want."

Jenita Cargile, a confidential investigator in Los Angeles, concurs: "I generally plan everything I do in my head first. I don't care if it's baking a cake or whatever, I go through the whole process. In my kind of work, I might have to drop something in the middle if someone comes and wants me to do surveillance. So I'm flexible and it never throws me off. I can change my mind in a split second and go on to something else and it doesn't bother me at all. This way I don't get upset and think my whole day is ruined because something I planned doesn't get done."

Ironically, many of the best planners we talked to do not consider themselves good planners because they have not scheduled every minute. But it's this flexibility that ranks them among the best of planners, not the worst.

Family service agency worker Rosemary Gaillard, another very active woman, believes that *life is what happens while you're busy making plans:* "I want *now* to be productive enough that if in a year or two I feel strongly I want to be doing something different, then I can go after that. I don't want to set a big huge goal and then wear myself out getting to it, losing a sense of the quality of *now*."

Her daily plans reflect this need for flexibility: "One of my projects which I hope to accomplish by the end of September is to slap a couple of coats of paint on my daughter's walls. I don't say 'OK, Tuesday night I'm going to come home and paint Tracy's room.' I just know that that's something I want to do and if I feel like it Tuesday night, I'll do it; if I don't, I won't."

Gaillard resists the concept of planning in the abstract, yet her very ability to think of planning in her terms is what enables her to plan and to get things done without racing around like a forever wound-up robot. If she said "OK, Tuesday night I'm going to paint Tracy's room no matter what," she wouldn't be allowing for interruptions, pleasant or otherwise. Any interruption could throw her entire schedule off. It'd be a house of cards, and we know what happens to those, right?

## DEALING WITH THE UNEXPECTED

Planning is a flexible schedule that gives you time to do the musts, with extra time for the unexpected.

Judy Sommerschield pinpoints what's wrong with trying to

control your own time totally: "You might be able to organize your own time, but you *cannot* organize other people's time effectively. And because you deal with other people, their inability to organize their time perhaps encroaches on your management of your own time."

If we were able to *totally control our time*, we could perhaps afford a minute-by-minute schedule. But outside influences invariably disrupt us, so we must build in time for such disruptions. This is only being realistic, and unless we're realistic we can't get time under our control.

Barbara Kulicke, the New York framing business owner, calls it "survival planning on an immediate level and on a long-range level. You can do it both ways, if you're a chess player. I often describe myself as playing a three-dimensional chess game."

## WHY RESIST IT?

Dr. Doris Moss recognizes resistance to planning: "I think sometimes it's better not to be overly analytical about things and not label and categorize things in ways that make them unpalatable or less attractive. You can't say 'Well, now I'm into my food management accountability' at home. It's better not to label it, just let it happen, make it part of your day. There will be a lot less resentment. I don't think that structure precludes spontaneity. It's all in how we view it."

If you insist on regarding planning as rigid because it sounds like such a stern word, it *is* going to be very intimidating and create new anxieties in place of old ones that time management can eradicate. If you accept planning as a flexible tool to gain more control of your time, it's going to be much easier to welcome the idea into your life.

Carol Bellamy, the New York City Council president who, because of her aversion to lateness, might logically be considered somewhat inflexible, proves just the opposite: "Government gives you the opportunity to have an enormously flexible schedule. I think it's important. But I don't think it's terrible that you have certain set times for things that have to be done. You can work around these. I don't think you should think you've done some disastrous thing by canceling something or having to shift it, as long as it doesn't become a pattern; and as long as being late doesn't become a pattern."

So keep in mind that time management for the many, many roles of women depends on flexibility, and planning is not a set of handcuffs. There's help:

The to-do list may be the road map of life, but nobody says you can't take any side trips.

# Tips for Time-Conscious Women Travelers

WITH 40 million women in the work force, more and more of us are embarking on that previously romanticized male lark, the business trip.

Women traveling on business now make up 25 percent of the travel market in this country—it was 8 percent just seven years ago. United Airlines announced in 1979 that 18 percent, nearly one in five, of its business travelers were women, as compared to an untraceable percentage eight years ago. The number of women taking business trips is increasing at a rate three times as fast as the figures for men; more than 3 million women spent more than $12 billion for 32 million nights on the road in 1977.

As we put this mileage behind us we find that the business trip isn't so romantic after all, particularly when you must still cope with being a mother and wife at the same time you're a thousand miles away because of business commitments.

Good time management puts a little pleasure into such trips; we'll divide your strategies into three stages: before, during, and after.

## BEFORE TRIPS

If you've already given your subordinates and your family the benefit of your delegation skills, you can count on this being a time when it truly pays off. Things run much more smoothly in your absence when left in the hands of people who know how to run them in your presence.

Supplement day-to-day responsibilities with clear instructions, written and verbal, on what needs to be accomplished and taken care of while you're away; then you can concentrate on the business of the trip.

## GETTING READY AT HOME

To prepare at home you'll also want to:

Make arrangements for care of children with a ready backup arrangement.

Leave a list of emergency numbers with the person who will care for your children, including school name and telephone number, teacher's name, doctor, helpful neighbor.

Tell children's teachers you'll be out of town for a certain number of days.

If school money will be needed or special functions are taking place, leave an envelope with instructions.

Leave a written list of all instructions: bedtime, eating habits, special medication, or problems that occur regularly.

Leave a copy of your itinerary. *Let children know you can be reached at all times* and that you'll be calling at regularly scheduled times.

Remind children of their responsibilities around the house, and that you expect them to be carried out in your absence.

Plan ahead for anything that can go wrong. It is overplanning which will give you peace of mind later.

## GETTING READY AT WORK

To prepare at work you'll want to:

Make sure the office staff has a copy of your itinerary and where you can be reached at all times.

Plan ahead for any projects that must be completed before the trip.

Leave enough time before the trip to complete and review all material for the trip. Remember: Anything that can go wrong, will.

If material needed for the trip has been sent to an outside source (e.g., a printer or lawyer), make sure it's back in your office several days before the trip. The day you leave is not when you want to find out that the printer cannot meet deadlines or that there is an error.

Check everything you're taking on the trip. If you're using slides, run through the presentation to ensure that all slides are right side up. Do you have enough handouts? Are your tape recorder batteries working?

Delegate activities that should be worked on while you are away. Make sure everyone knows what's expected of them.

Train staff well in advance so they can handle crises in your absence. Try to anticipate problems that may surface.

Take along an ample supply of business cards for new contacts you may meet.

Carry writing pads, pencils, film, calculator—whatever you

need in your business. Don't count on a store being open at the other end.

Don't wait until the last minute to get tickets. All reservations should have a written confirmation.

This last point brings up a service that's almost too good to be true. It's *free* and not always taken advantage of by novice travelers: the travel agency.

If your company does not have in-house capabilities and expects you to make your own reservations, a travel agent can save you enormous amounts of time and money. If this is your first trip to a certain place, tell the agent. Give the agent all your plans, and tell her your likes, dislikes, and needs. Ask for advice on climate, transportation, prices.

This is an excellent investment of time which enables the agent to make your trip as smooth as possible, such as selecting a hotel near your meetings. Of course, as with all delegation, be prepared to review everything the agent has done for you *before* leaving on the trip.

Remember the service is free. Travel agents are paid a commission by the transportation industry.

## THE ART OF PACKING

Good packing habits will also save time and energy when traveling.

If traveling is a regular part of your career, consider keeping a duplicate set of toiletries and traveling needs in a separate dresser drawer, in a travel kit, or in your suitcase—items such as small bottles of makeup, perfume, deodorant, travel iron, travel alarm, sewing kit, mirror, wash and dry packets, Woolite packets, electric coil to heat water for tea or coffee, folding travel umbrella, travel toothbrush, toothpaste, and any other item you use daily. Duplication saves packing and unpacking time, and leaves items available at home where they may be needed by others.

Suitcases should be as lightweight as possible. Most regular women travelers have learned to pack just enough to fit in a case that they can carry aboard and either hang in the front of the plane or keep under the seat (height plus length plus width equals maximum 45 inches); that saves time at the baggage claim. Clothes, therefore, should be minimal and versatile, in basic styles and colors. Try the layered look if traveling to places with different climates; you can peel as it gets warmer or add layers as it gets cooler. Coordinate clothes so different outfits can be made out of a few basics. Choose comfortable, well-fitting clothes of fabrics that need little care and do not crease and wrinkle easily. Always take an extra pair of panty hose for emergencies.

A travel iron may seem like a nuisance, but it's much lighter than extra clothes would be.

## MAKING WAITING PAY

Waiting time always seems to go hand in hand with travel: waiting in the airport, waiting for meetings, traffic delays, and so forth. Make sure you have material (work or leisure) to see you through waiting periods. It's a great time to catch up on junk mail, dictate correspondence to your secretary (mail the cassette with prestamped envelopes), write personal letters, enjoy the latest best-seller.

## DURING TRIPS

Flexibility is especially valuable in traveling schedules. You'll find yourself in strange towns with different customs, uncharted routes, and various pressures and raised expectations.

Prepare for the unexpected by building even more flexibility into your schedule than usual. The temptation, when traveling for business, is to cram as many functions and appointments as possible into the little time you have.

Be reasonable or you may find the trip blowing up because of overcommitments.

When traveling by car, plan the trip realistically so you don't arrive exhausted.

Allow enough time to get to airports on time; when you arrive, orient yourself about the layout, ticket counters, baggage claim. Each airport is different and, as Betty Harragan notes, "It never occurs to airline people that people take airplanes; there is not one thing to indicate that there are people in the place." It can take a fast-paced 20 minutes to get from car to plane, not including ticket pickup, so be prepared.

Airline clubs such as American Airlines' Admiral Club; TWA's Ambassador Club; and Pan American's Clipper Club all require a membership fee, but the benefits can be worth it to you. The hostess will check on your ticket and give you your boarding pass; cocktail lounges are part of the package; messages can be delivered to you; telephones for business calls are available; and the ambience is conducive to women traveling alone.

## CREDIT CARD MAGIC

The rent-a-car stations are always near the baggage claim area and credit cards for specific firms—Hertz, Avis, Budget, or whatever—will save you huge amounts of time, even if you wince at owning another credit card. The firms keep forms on file containing all information needed, so renting a car involves only a quick phone call. You save even more time when dropping a car off; the credit card number enables you to leave the car and fill out all drop-off forms later at your convenience, rather than having to wait in line and fear you'll miss your plane. The card also proves invaluable in towns where an agency might close early, leaving you wondering whether to shoot your car.

Speaking of credit cards, general cards (Master Charge, Visa, American Express, Carte Blanche, and so forth) can also be time-savers. Having your plane delayed an hour can be turned into an advantage by using the time to shop: a credit card makes this possible when you're not carrying extra money with you. Each company offers various services, such as American Express's assured reservations (call ahead, give your card number, ask for an assured reservation, and the room will be waiting for you until checkout time next day); or the ability to borrow money or cash checks with the card (particularly valuable when you run out of cash in a strange city).

Limousine services, either hotel or airport, are an alternative to taxis and rental cars, especially if all your business will be at or near your hotel.

Get a map of the city, checking out directions to appointments enough in advance to allow for unexpected traveling distances. If you will be using local transportation, find out schedules, fare, special information.

*187*

Always carry change for fares and tips; 50 cents may seem like small change to you but it'll get you where you're going faster in the hands of a bellman or airport porter.

When you arrive at the hotel, tell them you're there on business and that you need all calls and messages directed to you immediately. Ask about valet service, room service, and other services available. If you'll need an ironing board, ask for one on check-in, since they may be limited. Most hotels are only too happy to make you happy, particularly when they know there's a possibility of your becoming a regular patron, so if you need something, *ask*. They can usually help you with reasonable requests. And more hotels are automatically including women-oriented services and conveniences such as good makeup lighting in the bathroom, special shopping services, female concierges, and skirt hangers.

## AFTER TRIPS

Coming home is that much easier if prior planning has been effective. There'll always be things that couldn't get done in your absence, but if minor details and daily work have been handled, your first day back on the job or at home will not be as hectic as it will be if nothing has been done in your absence.

The plane trip home is a good time to sort out results of your trip and expectations of what awaits you at home and in the office.

## GOOD DEALS FOR WOMEN

Women who travel regularly agree that—except for minor inconveniences men have been facing for years, such as the phone near the bed instead of the desk, and no skirt (or pants) hangers—travel conditions have improved tremendously in the past few years, and continue to improve as the industry becomes more aware of women travelers and intent on profiting from the market.

The one problem all women have in common, and that there is no absolute answer for, is the concern they feel about leaving their children at home.

While Betty Harragan was able to take her one child along when she was younger, taking more than one is not feasible; and it's totally impractical when a child is older and must attend school.

What these women have settled on to ease their concern is extremely detailed planning: lists, itineraries, notifying neighbors and teachers. But the most important requirement to them is letting their children know that they can be reached at all times. "Mother is only a phone call away" goes a long way to reassure children who might view a thousand-mile distance skeptically.

A major advantage of the business trip is the ability to combine business with pleasure, time and situation permitting. Marie McDonald is one of many women who is able to arrange vacation time in conjunction with the elevator industry conventions she attends each year; and her husband comes along for the enjoyment.

Careful planning, such as knowing long in advance when and where the conventions fall each year, will enable you to put such business/travel time to pleasurable use.

Once again, *planning is the key* to comfortable, effective business travel. For example, when possible it's faster and happier not to travel with the crowd. Try not to go during rush hours, especially Monday mornings, and Friday evenings. Peak times are hassle times and enormous time-wasters, and that includes Miami in winter and San Francisco all summer. By considering potential mishaps in advance you can probably forestall 98 percent of the problems, making the other 2 percent much easier to cope with.

# Here's Time Just for You

When I was pregnant, someone told me that something
would have to go. I turned to Michael and said, "I just
can't imagine what would go! Everything is critical; it's
already pared to the bone." I went through my whole
repertoire. And what went was time for me.

—CINDY ANNCHILD
*Co-owner, the Bath House*

Leisure is as good for you as vitamins or sleep. If it will
help you to kick the guilt habit, look at it this way:
You owe it to your work, your family, and yourself.

—KATE RAND LLOYD
*Editor,* Working Woman

WHENEVER I ASK WOMEN about time for themselves, the
reply is nearly always identical: "Time for *me*?"

Exasperated, puzzled, resigned, humorous—no matter how
they view the subject and no matter how well or poorly planned
their lives are, most women regard time for themselves as more
or less unreal.

For one woman, "time for me" may mean being able to
spend many hours a day working in her own business; for another, it may mean luxuriating in bed every other Sunday; for a
third, "it could be the hour each night spent uninterrupted with
her children.

Time for you is time that you've determined to be most important to you for your *fun,* relaxation, enjoyment.

Working long hours at a job may not be "time for me" to one woman, and a day in bed may not be to another. But it's important to recognize the difference between *choosing* your own time and being forced to do something and *accepting* it as your own time.

If you don't make time for yourself, the person you were before you became a career woman (or before you became a wife and mother) gets lost. We must all maintain our self-identity, our uniqueness, without becoming lost in the other roles we assume.

If you're working 18 hours a day, as I was, and you hate it, as I eventually did, do something about it! Ask yourself what you'd *like* to be doing, and begin setting your priorities to include time for yourself. Whatever you select, time for yourself should serve one major purpose: It should permit you to do something you consider being good to yourself.

## NOBODY WILL DO IT FOR YOU

Women, traditionally the caretakers, must take care of themselves; nobody else will. The women I know who are the happiest are those who reward themselves with gifts of time, either occasionally or regularly. The disassatisfied women put themselves last, and if there's any leftover time at the end of the day, week, or year, they feel guilty spending it on themselves.

"We know the old saw," says Dr. Doris Moss, "about being frustrated, feeling unfulfilled, and resenting your time at home. You're going to be a lot less effective in your role as mother and wife than if you're feeling good about what you're doing, something you're excited about. You may come home at the end of the day, maybe a little tired, but feeling good and bubbly and up, knowing that it really was a great day. The kind of time you then spend with your husband and children will be better than the hours you have spent with them feeling dissastisfied about yourself."

A woman who chooses work as her own time, Dr. Moss says, is doing OK as long as it works for her: "Her flexibility is to decide to be inflexible. No one can say 'You have to have leisure time and you have to enjoy it. Whether you want to or not, you'd better read this book and relax and listen to music and paint your toenails.' But those who think they do want such time for themselves and want to do all those things have to evolve some kind of system to make time, just as they do for everything else. *You make time!* But we still find it very hard to believe that we're not indispensable, either to our careers or to our people at home. It's very hard to say 'I'm taking an hour' or 'I'm taking a day' or 'I'm taking a week' or whatever—nothing's going to happen if you do.

"If someone doesn't have any leisure, any fun hours, something's wrong."


## IT'S VERY DIFFERENT FOR WOMEN

Knowing that you should have leisure time doesn't relieve all the conflicts that make it nearly impossible for you to find such time, right? So what do you do? *These daily conflicts are what makes time management a different proposition for women than for men.* External and internal conflicts relentlessly wear at us and constantly force us to make difficult choices.

Although we cannot eliminate many of our pulls and tugs,

we can minimize their counterproductive, time-wasting effects.

The internal conflicts, of course, are based on our own feelings that we must be Superwoman and the feelings of guilt that wear us down when we don't live up to our image of Superwoman. Once we realize it's acceptable to leave the dishes in the sink if we're exhausted or to get to the halfway point on our to-do list and run out of the day, then we're better able to cope with external conflicts.

Encouragingly, the working woman's conflict between job and home and all the attendant problems are finally being recognized by the rest of society. Change is always gradual, but the past few years have brought undeniable improvement.

Stores are staying open later to accommodate the working woman who can no longer shop during daytime hours.

More companies are selling by mail and phone.

Delivery services are increasing.

Banks are computerizing and becoming accessible 24 hours (no more banker's hours).

Husbands are beginning to share in housework and child-care responsibilities; some husbands are demanding to share them (others are more reluctant).

NOW, the feminist organization, has targeted the family and its importance for its challenge of the '80s: ". . . to frame a new agenda that makes it possible for women to be able to work and love in equality with men—and to choose, if they so desire, to have children," as Betty Friedan wrote in the *New York Times Magazine*. "Even the measure of equality we have already achieved is not secure until we face the unanticipated conflicts between the demands of the workplace and professional success on the one hand, and the demands of the family on the other. These conflicts seem insoluble because of the way the family and workplace have been structured in America."

Friedan called for changes in societal traditions (such as child care, office hours, and other institutions) to conform with the already changed family structure, changed by the working woman.

This amounts to a general recognition that the mental and physical health of more than half the population is at stake because of these constant conflicts. An updated mental health survey conducted by the National Center for Health Statistics shows that today more women in their 20s and 30s are suffering from stress.

Another study (by the Security Pacific National Bank of Los Angeles) notes that "currently, 80 percent of all families earning $20,000 or more are two-wage-earner families. Two wage earners place less emphasis on careers and increased value on leisure activities, child care, and household services. Career roles are less instrumental than the search for self-identity and good health."

The times, they truly are a-changin'. And while working women may reap the benefits of the changes that have already materialized (time-saving products, 24-hour services, flextime corporations, increased child-care options), we must still contend with much that's not yet changed and still creates the old conflicts that keep us from considering time for ourselves as a priority.

## YOU'RE THE PRIORITY YOURSELF!

Back to the original question: Where do I get this time for me?

The obvious answer is to *make* yourself a priority and *make* the time for yourself just as you *make* the time for anything else you consider important.

But, you say, it's so much easier to eliminate the "time for me" if anything unexpected occurs.

That's true. But let's consider the results of no time for you. More and more women are being admitted to hospitals with heart attacks at younger ages (no national figures are available yet, it's such a recent trend); more women are suffering from stress. And women are definitely frustrated and unhappy because they have no leisure time—however they may define leisure—and families do pick up these feelings.

Though leisure time is first to go when something must give, a 1979 study, the National Survey of Working Women conducted by the National Commission on Working Women, found that "lack of leisure time was considered the most serious concern for employed women, 53 percent (of 110,000 responses)."

If you're one of the thousands (more probably millions) of women who want leisure time and don't know how to get it and probably don't even think it's there to get, it's time to take another look at your priorities.

The key to time for you is the key to all time management: yes, again, planning, overall and daily. Just as you plan your career goals; plan your day's agenda; plan time for your family; plan to allow for spontaneity; so you must plan time that's reserved just for you. If you don't, it just will not happen, that's all!

Women who seem to accomplish a great deal all have two things in common: They plan time for themselves, and they do it without guilt.

"There is nothing more important to me," says Rosemary Gaillard, who works at a family service agency, "in the situation that I'm in, and I think probably for the rest of my life—there will be nothing more important to me than my emotional and psychological health. I'll take care of that first. I feel if that's not in good shape, nothing is. If I really need time for me, I take it. And I don't feel the tiniest bit of guilt about taking it. If I really need time and don't take it, then nothing else works well."

"A lot of women feel that it's a mortal sin to be good to themselves," says Rose Gruppuso, co-owner of Gruppuso Plumbing, "because first is your husband, if you have one, and then is your children, and then your house and then, if there's any pennies left, then you come. Well, that's the wrong attitude, because lying in that hospital bed [she had a serious operation eleven years ago] I realized that the most important thing to me is me. If I'm important to me, then everyone else is going to come very easy; I'm going to take care of everyone else and love everyone else and do for everyone else if I'm happy with me and I can take care of me. It's too bad we've been brought up not to think of ourselves."

If scares about stress and heart attacks bore you, perhaps the perceptions of these women will convince you of the importance of time for you.

## HOW YOU CAN PRACTICE

Much has been made of the "me decade," the '70s. You may think that time for you is just another excuse to be selfish; it is! But isn't it also selfish not to indulge yourself and then take it out on your family and co-workers, maybe even with an attitude of "Look how much I'm sacrificing for you"? No one appreciates *that* kind of self-indulgence, which is exactly what guilt and self-pity and (at its extreme) martyrdom are.

You owe it to yourself and to those around you to be good to yourself.

You'll find time to be good to yourself by practicing:

1. *The basics of time management as discussed: These include*—

- Good communication
- Compromising (or balancing) perfectionist standards
- Delegating at home and at work
- Valuing your time as money and paying for services and products
- Learning to say no
- Recognizing (and eliminating) daily time-wasters such as telephone and drop-in interruptions; uncontrolled television time; excessive meetings; continuing crises; personal disorganization
- Making use of personal networks
- Turning waiting time into profitable time—leisure, thinking, whatever
- Keeping a daily to-do list and continually updating priorities

2. *Your quality-of-life values*: I'll show you how to set these in the next section, but in two words, they're your *life plan* which enables you to mesh your conflicts so it 'll no longer always be a tug-of-war: husband versus work, children versus work, you versus work. All the daily conflicts that keep you from finding time for yourself can mesh with time for yourself and ways to find even further time for yourself—time alone, time for vacations, and so forth.

Without the overall quality-of-life values a resolution of these conflicts is next to impossible. Choosing your values won't be easy, but it'll become progressively more natural if you continue to reevaluate your plans, goals, and priorities.

And if you still sometimes feel twinges when you place yourself first, take some advice from Rosemary Gaillard: "It does take some work, some time to get past feeling guilty about it. I think the one thing I've had to fight—and a lot of women have had to fight—is that I owe everybody else my energy but myself."

# How to Find Your
# Quality-of-Life Values

I have some fantasies that are wonderful; I don't know
if I could really make them come true.
—SUSAN SCHEIN
*Owner of public relations firm*

WHILE CONDUCTING SEMINARS in time management and
during the research for this book, I noticed an interesting tendency among the women I met. Asked to write down their lifetime *goals,* they seemed to freeze, unable to think of specific
goals they would want to commit to paper. Gradually, I began
rephrasing the exercise:

"Fantasize," I urged; "write down whatever motivates you,
the things that make up your dreams, what you really want out
of life."

The women found it much easier to express dreams, and once
they let themselves go they listed an endless number of *values;*
family relationships, financial security, career/business dreams,
power, success, achievement, social and recreational activities,
health, assertiveness, order, peacefulness . . .

So I started a different way to set lifetime goals. It lets you
recognize your *lifetime values* first. Then you set goals compati-

ble with those values. Now lifetime goal setting becomes much easier; it's not hard for me or for the women I counsel to reconcile our daily and yearly goals with our desired quality-of-life values.

This is true for women (less so for men) because the multiplicity of our conflicts is understandably bewildering. We panic when asked to set even the first all-inclusive goal: What should come first? Career? Children? Money? Sexual relationships?

But when we first recognize what we want our personal quality of life to be (or what it *must* be for a while) we find it easier to set specific goals.

## HOW TO PICK YOUR QUALITY-OF-LIFE VALUES

At this point, take time for the following exercise:

Write down a list of values that motivate you, all you dream about and wish for constantly (see samples below).

Look at your list. What's the most important quality-of-life value to you? Mark that "A" for primary value, then go through the list and determine second, third, fourth values and so on.

If you have second thoughts about any of your choices, change the order until you feel you have accurately identified your quality-of-life priorities.

Your list may look like this:

1. Family.
2. Career.
3. Good friendships.
4. Financial security.

Or it may look like this:

1. Career.
2. Financial security.
3. Friendships.
4. Family.

The first could well be the list of a person who has small children and feels that her current priorities naturally lie with them; the second list may be that of a single woman who wants to concentrate on establishing herself professionally before starting a family.

In any event, you'll want to understand why your values are what they are, and that the list is not necessarily permanent.

*Lifetime values change with time,* just as your life itself changes.

The situations determining the current value may change (your family grows older and you no longer need to spend so much time with them); or you achieve your primary value and can concentrate on the next (your career is going great and you're ready to begin your family without interrupting the career). Physician's secretary Susan Friedman's values and goals changed often even within one year:

"I've only been divorced a year. I've found that in the last year I've sat down and made long-range plans a lot because as things have changed in my life my goals have changed. My immediate goal was financial security, to make sure I was going to make it at all. My next goal was to make sure my daughter was getting the things she needed. And now my goal is to go back to graduate school because those other two things have been accomplished."

As with Friedman, your life values may be determined by necessity; in her case, financial security obviously had to come first. Women with small children often plan their life values around their families, knowing that if push comes to shove the family takes precedence anyway.

The list you have just made should determine what values are most important in your life right now, and will probably be much the same for the next five years.

## HOW GOALS HELP ATTAIN QUALITY-OF-LIFE VALUES

Now you can set goals that will lead you to your life values. The goals are specific aspects of the values you've identified; naturally, you'll want them to be consistent—they're stepping-stones.

If "family relationships" leads your life values list, for example, you should not set career development as your top goal; that would undermine your primary value. You *can* work on more than one life value at a time, but you'll want to recognize your priorities; secondary life values should come second or goal conflicts will develop.

If family is your primary value, you wouldn't choose a career path requiring a great deal of travel or constant absence from your family. If career is primary, you won't set goals for community projects that would interfere with career development.

Often, luckily, steps we take to reach one goal will help in reaching another. My serving on the board of directors for the New York Association of Women Business Owners not only helped my community goal by enabling me to serve the community in projects I worked on for the association; it also proved invaluable in making business contacts, which was consistent with my business goals.

When I've been asked to join other organizations I kept a very clear picture of my goals in mind and was able to determine what would be the best for those goals and channel my energy in the best possible, most effective direction.

On a fresh sheet of paper, write down your primary quality-of-life value. Then list the goals you have set for that quality.

EXAMPLE: FAMILY (Value). Goals:

1. Spend more time with children.
2. Spend more time with husband.
3. Improve relationship with mother.
4. Plan family reunion.

Now determine the most important goal on this list. This'll be the goal you want to do something about right now.


## LIST ACTIVITIES YOU CAN DO TO ATTAIN THE GOAL

Since a goal is not an activity, you need to plan doable activities to help you reach the goal.

After determining your goal, ask yourself what you can do to achieve it. List all the steps you can take.

Sometimes it helps to ask yourself:

"Why don't I have _____?" ("Why don't I have *more time with the children?*")

The question, like the time log, pinpoints specific problems, such as "We're watching too much television, and don't talk" or "The phone is constantly interrupting us."

Being aware of what's keeping you from your goals helps you to take specific action to remedy the situation: setting time limits on television viewing or taking the phone off the hook *during* certain time periods.

The question, "Why don't I have _____?" has proved as valuable as the original Silcox question in determining where my time problems are and how to overcome them.

## YOUR OWN TIMETABLE

The next step in the strategy is to determine a timetable for your activities. We all know the problem about good intentions: the road to hell is paved with them. Since we want our road to lead somewhere else, we pave it with something other than good intentions—concrete blocks of action.

Timing is important. First write down the date you plan to get into action on the first activity; then the deadline for achieving the goal, which puts it in sight.

Instead of sighing "Tomorrow is another day" (and I've always thought that if Clark Gable was getting away from *me*, I certainly wouldn't wait another day), make up a list of self-imposed deadlines.

This isn't supposed to put pressure on you, much less create new anxieties; it'll spread out a realistic overview of what you want to accomplish. And you'll definitely want to be realistic about the times you put down.

## THINK NOW, PROFIT FOREVER

Establishing your life values and the goals and activities that will lead you to these values is not (like the to-do list) a push-pull-click-click deal. You should spend time on this overview of your life and consider this time a blue-ribbon investment; it'll pay off handsomely for years and years in time you'll save and values you'll achieve.

I think it's wise to have several quality-of-life values, complete with goals and activities, running concurrently, as long as you keep your priorities straight.

Given the conflicts all women face, such an overview of values will enable you to begin to weave them together daily, turning conflicts into complementary roles, making them work *for* and *with* each other, not *against*.

Judy Sommerschield (owner of Schield Personnel), who uses a similar method, finds that it eases her conflicts—husband, children, two businesses, self—immensely:

"My husband and I try to set goals together when all of a sudden we're feeling very frustrated or very unable to cope. We sometimes feel we're going in the wrong direction and we'll try to sit back and say what are our first priorities and what can we forget so we can accomplish our first priorities, yet have some leisure time too?

"The major goal now is to have enough time to have a family life with our two children so we can instill in them the type of character we choose. Business goals are important because we own our own business, although my husband works elsewhere. So that's next in importance. Then we have goals in redecorating our new home. We list things that must be accomplished at work and things that must be accomplished at home—and forget all the extraneous things, putting them off to another year or another time. So now we'll have more time to go bike riding. We set goals and priorities periodically, about every four to six months, because that's about the time we realize we're getting bogged down."

Every four to six months is a good time to reevaluate values and reestablish goals and activities; do it no less than once a year.

Whether you're bogged down or not, this will keep everything fresh and allow you to incorporate changes, both subtle and obvious. (As activities for your goals finish, establish a new goal for the quality-of-life value, and start the process from the top.)

Your reviews keep you in touch with your progress without being overwhelmed, and let you keep your daily planning and priority setting on the right track.

On completion of the exercises in this section, with your entire life plan laid out neatly before you, it's very tempting to try to accomplish everything at once.

Warning: Don't!

You'll only defeat the purpose of time management, which is to learn how to use your time well, not abuse it. Take it slowly at first; you'll be surprised at the momentum generated by your honest evaluations, careful planning, and realistic deadlines. (Sample quality-of-life charts follow.)

# QUALITY-OF-LIFE GOALS

EXAMPLE:

Date: _____

My Quality-of-Life Values are:

|    |                            | Priority |
|----|----------------------------|----------|
| 1. | Career/business            | 2        |
| 2. | Financial security         | 3        |
| 3. | Family relationships       | 1        |
| 4. | Recreational activities    | 5        |
| 5. | Success                    | 6        |
| 6. | Health/physical well-being | 4        |
| 7. | Good friendships           | 7        |
| 8. | Spiritual values           | 9        |
| 9. | Achievement                | 10       |
| 10.| Independence               | 8        |

Date: _____

My Quality-of-Life Values Are:

Priority

1.

2.

3.

4.

5.

6.

7.

8.

9.

10.

PRIMARY QUALITY-OF-LIFE GOAL: FAMILY RELATIONSHIPS

GOAL: Spend more time with children

Activities:
1. Thursday night is family night
2. Take each child out alone to talk
3. Have no interruptions during meals
4. Watch less TV
5. Plan family picnic for July 4

SECOND QUALITY-OF-LIFE GOAL: CAREER/BUSINESS

GOAL: Increase sales of department by 35 percent

Activities:
1. Work with sales staff to increase efficiency
2. Review old client list; see why not reordering
3. Develop sales campaign
4. See what competitors are doing

THIRD QUALITY-OF-LIFE GOAL: FINANCIAL SECURITY

GOAL: Have $5,000 in savings account by 12/15/80

Activities:
1. Put $_____ in account each week
2. Review budget; cut down expenses
3. Consolidate bills
4. Research fuel-saving devices

FOURTH QUALITY-OF-LIFE GOAL: HEALTH/PHYSICAL WELL-BEING

GOAL: Lose ten pounds by 10/80

Activities:
1. Start diet tomorrow
2. Join exercise program
3. Walk instead of taking car
4. Climb stairs, forget elevators
5. Plan menu with less fattening food
6. Take lunch to work, avoid impulse lunches

QUALITY-OF-LIFE VALUE: FAMILY

GOAL: Spend more time with the children

| | Start | By When |
|---|---|---|
| 1.   Block off Thursday night to spend with family | 6/30 | Regularly 7/14 |
| 2a. Plan day alone with Johnny | 7/3 | Regularly 8/1 |
| 2b. Plan day alone with Sandy | 7/10 | Regularly 8/7 |
| 3.   Have no interruptions during meals—phone, visits | immed. | |
| 4.   Watch less TV | | |
| 5.   Plan family picnic for July 4 | Tuesday | 7/4 |
| | | |
| | | |
| | | |
| | | |

YOUR QUALITY-OF-LIFE VALUE:

YOUR GOAL:

| | Start | By When |
|---|---|---|
| | | |
| | | |
| | | |
| | | |
| | | |
| | | |
| | | |
| | | |
| | | |
| | | |

# Setting Your Career Goals

I was starting the business at the same time I was starting a family—which is poor timing.

—MARGO BERK-LEVINE
*Employment agency owner*

SETTING CAREER GOALS is crucial if you're a working woman with a family, because it'll help mesh your multiroles and smooth the way in each department by reducing friction as much as possible.

When I ask working women how they got where they are today in their careers they'll say "By chance," "Pure luck," "I sort of fell into it," "I just happened to be in the right place at the right time . . ."

This is usually accurate; since women are new in the work force, we've tended to take what we can get and work from there. Frequently this haphazard career "management" pays off as we advance or branch out into fields that attract our attention.

But as women begin to view working as a right, not a privilege, many of us are no longer content just to take what we can get. We have definite interests and definite ideas of where we want to go, how much we want to be earning, what we want to contribute.

Enter career goal setting:

Mapping a strategy for careers is vital if we're not going to founder in a mass of details waiting for "luck," which will not get us very far. As with anything else, unless we know where we're going, we're not going to get there.

When you first begin setting your career goals, keep in mind your overall life values and priorities. If your immediate priority is your family, your career needn't be relegated to a back burner. Margo Berk-Levine is a prime example of a woman who was able to build her employment agency at the same time she built her family. She did it by making her priorities work *for* her. Since family and business were her top priorities, she began unloading other duties. She hired a housekeeper, delegated more responsibility at work, etc.

## WHERE DO YOU WANT TO BE?

Having established and recognized your priorities, begin setting your goals by asking yourself the question:

*Where do I want to be five years from now?*

List each five-year goal. You may only have one or you may have several. *Be realistic* about the time frame. The easiest way to establish a realistic time frame is to break the five-year plan down into more manageable time periods. Ask yourself:

*Where should I be in two years if I'm going to be ———— in five?*

If, for example, your five-year plan calls for your becoming vice-president of your company, your two-year plan might see you as manager of your department.

Breaking down your five-year plan will enable you—

- To see if your deadlines for the overall five-year plan are realistic
- To concentrate on specific steps needed to attain your goals

- To recognize whether your goals are compatible with your life values as well as your established priorities
- To practice the "baby step" method in its purest form: taking an overwhelming five-year *objective* and translating it into practical doable *activities*

Then continue goal setting with additional questions and lists:
*What are the most important things I can do in my job within the next 12 months?*
*Within the next six months ?*
*What are my A priorities for the next two months?*
Essentially, goal setting requires that you—

- Position assumptions, conditions or premises that clarify the goal and are specific about what the goal is

    (Establish the validity of these premises. For example, "I want to establish a plan for recruiting engineers next year." Validity is shown by research which has proved there will be more engineers in the job market next year. The success of planning depends on these assumptions, but do recognize that some conditions are uncontrollable, e.g., reduction in labor turnover.)
- Research the facts, data, and other information
- Analyze those facts
- Establish assumptions that appear reasonable
- Develop alternative plans; establish pros and cons
- Select the best plan for action—incorporate timing, specifications, a control system; identify resources
- Act after communicating with your superiors and subordinates; choose how you'll proceed and who'll be responsible for what

Sample charts follow.

## GOALS: TWO MONTHS TO FIVE YEARS FROM NOW

### WHERE DO I WANT TO BE FIVE YEARS FROM NOW?

1.

2.

3.

4.

5.

6.

7.

### WHERE SHOULD I BE IN TWO YEARS SO I CAN MEET MY FIVE-YEAR PLAN?

1.

2.

3.

4.

5.

6.

7.

## WHAT ARE THE MOST IMPORTANT THINGS I CAN DO IN MY JOB WITHIN THE NEXT 12 MONTHS?

1.

2.

3.

4.

5.

6.

7.

8.

9.

10.

11.

12.

13.

14.

15.

## WHAT ARE MY "A" PRIORITIES FOR THE NEXT TWO MONTHS?

1.

2.

3.

4.

5.

6.

7.

8.

9.

10.

## LIST ACTIVITIES TO OBTAIN GOAL NUMBER ONE:

1.

2.

3.

4.

5.

6.

7.

8.

9.

10.

## GETTING WHERE YOU'RE GOING

Once you have your overall plan, you can rely on your daily to-do lists and priority setting to get where you're going. The process becomes natural, because you're aware of your overall objective and what doables you need daily to achieve it.

Women resist setting goals for the same reason they resist making plans or lists: they fear the "inflexibility" of goal setting and the possibility of not reaching their goals in the time allotted.

Free-lance illustrator Genevieve Meek illustrates this anxiety: "My goals are so open-ended and personal. They're not the kind of goals you read about that women should set—like in five years

I want to be vice-president of Shell Oil. What I would really like to be is the very best illustrator in the city, the state, whatever I can get up to. I want to be good, and that's so open-ended that you can keep on working on it, I hope for a lifetime."

As in daily planning however, goal setting is only a direction to take, with no rule that you cannot take a side trip.

Rather than waiting around for luck to propel you forward, you're much more likely to succeed by working toward a specific goal. If something else comes along and distracts you from the original goal, it's time to reevaluate, not panic.

Cheryl Hughes, for example, on moving to the West Coast, tried desperately to get a job teaching, having set that as her goal. Eventually she took a job as an independent consultant, utilizing skills she learned while teaching. Her goal setting, centered on *now*, illustrates how flexible the process can be.

Illustrator Meek's goals are equally flexible—and just as valid as those of the woman who wants to be vice-president of a major oil company.

Reevaluation of goals (whether every three, six, or twelve months, depending on whatever proves necessary and workable for you) is vital. Without reviewing, we become so caught up in the singleminded intent of reaching our one goal that we lose sight of other opportunities. Reevaluation also eases another anxiety about setting goals: fear of not reaching them.

Since women are fairly new to goal setting, we tend to set unrealistic time limits. It is not unrealistic to aim for the presidency of your company, but it may be extremely unrealistic to make it your five-year objective.

When evaluating your goals, do look at—

- Your own progress toward that goal
- The prevailing conditions from sources other than yourself (office politics, recent vacancies, in-house shuffling . . .)
- Any changes in the direction you may wish to take

Reviewing all these points enables you to reset deadlines. There's no shame in pushing back a a self-imposed deadline that's impossible to meet. It's much worse to kill yourself trying to meet it and then miss it anyway.

Goal setting and reviewing should be regular, not just when you see something obvious has happened to change your direction. Subtle changes too often go unnoticed, and frequently they will shift your own direction.

Marie McDonald, who operates her own elevator company, illustrates the pitfalls of setting and evaluating goals only when embarking on large projects or when extremely busy: "I really hadn't done any goal setting until I started thinking about opening a company. And then the planning became very important. Once we had started the business, the pressure of work made it difficult to do much planning—there was just too much *doing*. When things began to let up, I didn't go back to the planning like I should have."

Planning in the way I've suggested shouldn't take much time out of busy days. By planning during busy times you're ensuring that you'll have profitable things to do during the not-so-busy periods. If you get so caught up in doing now-things that you can't plan for the future, the future may turn out to be depressingly unbusy, and you'll lose time then.

## YOU HAVE MORE EXPERIENCE THAN YOU THINK

No *goal* is impossible if you think you can attain it. Don't be deterred because it's never been done before or you didn't have formal training in the field.

Women must learn to make the most of their experience, to count it as valid when it applies to their careers, as it so very often does. Too many women downplay experience with the blanket self-putdown "I wasn't trained in it, so I guess I can't do it"—even if they've been doing it for five years.

Count everything—experience, training, reading, interaction with other people, general knowledge. If you know it or can do it, use it to reach your goals.

Hotel sales manager Donna Davis  who has been setting and reaching goals since she was eight (when she had her own lawn-mowing and pot holder enterprise), relies on this "generalization" process and uses whatever she learns to advance her career:

"If it had not been for my planning, I wouldn't have known how to negotiate my way up. It wasn't a matter of going in and taking the job and saying 'I want to do this.' It was a matter of saying 'This is what I want to do for this length of time, and I'm going to learn this part of the business, and then, once I do this, here's my next step. This is where I want to be next year at this time, and this is the amount of money I want to be making.' I went into the real estate business with that kind of attitude, and when I started in the hotel business, I did the same thing."

I also did the same thing: utilized everything I had learned from my work within large corporations to start my own business, originally intended to help other small companies get started, move their offices, design them, set up systems and procedures, train personnel. I had been doing all these things for the company I worked for and, though I had no *formal* training in setting up office systems, *I knew I could do it because I was doing it.*

When I realized where my talents lay, I began planning for my own business and establishing goals. Today, seven years later, the business has evolved differently, an example of how goal setting does not preclude change.

As I became more involved personally with time management, taking courses and doing all the research possible, I began to advise my clients on the subject; eventually the major portion of my business was devoted to time management.

Cindy Annchild, who had trouble setting goals, finally found a means to work on both personal and business goals. She joined a businesswomen's group to increase her knowledge of her own small business and began working with the other members on goal setting:

"The Bath Shop definitely needed planning ahead," she says. "I do it better in a group situation. It helps me get out of my details; you have to deal on the broader level."

If you have problems setting goals, do try working with someone else.

At first, let your fantasies take over to remove the mental block so many women have when trying to think of goals. Once the block has been removed, you'll probably find no end to goals. At this point, evaluate your priorities and begin setting realistic deadlines. Working with other people, either in a formal setting or with a friend or your husband, may help to get you away from the details we all get bogged down in.

Gradually, you'll be able to do it on your own, and you'll find yourself accomplishing much more by working toward something concrete than you will by waiting around for your lucky day.

# *Coping with Morning Madness*

I see no reason to go to work in a bad mood. There are enough things that come up at the last minute that you have to face. I don't see any reason for me to *make* problems to face.

— JACKIE FRISS
*Training specialist, New York State Education Department*

HOW YOU SPEND your mornings will set the tone for the rest of your day. Hectic, disorganized, busy mornings can put you in a bad mood before you even leave the house, much less get to work. Calm, fluid mornings can be a great start to a great day. Too many women are more familiar with the hectic variety than the calm. Time management can create great mornings.

When I did my time study for the Gillette Company (on how 300 women—working mothers, working singles, and nonworking mothers—spent time from when they got out of bed until they and/or the last child left the house) I found that many women were running around the house *without thinking about a strategy*.

Typically, women in the study would get up, run into the shower, put on a housecoat, go downstairs to the kitchen, start breakfast, go back upstairs, wake up the husband, go back downstairs, finish cooking and setting the table, go wake the children, do a little housework, throw in a load of wash, vacuum a little, go back upstairs, get dressed, and make the beds.

Mostly this uses up a lot of excess energy running around the house.

# I HATE MORNINGS!

Because I happen to be a terrible morning person, scarcely able to function for the first hour I'm awake, I was forced to supply myself with a strategy for every detail of those morning hours. So the night before I think about what I'll be doing the next day and what I should prepare for those planned activities.

If, for instance, I am going to teach a class after work, the night before I'll plan specifically what I'm going to need for the next day: extra files or clippings for my briefcase, a different set of clothes, that sort of thing. And I get those things ready the night before, because I'm aware that if I don't, I might forget them in the morning.

Result: I don't have to run around the house like a madwoman in the morning. The strategy is set: the routes I'm going to take throughout the house and what I'm going to do on the way to work if I have morning errands. But . . . I must do this every night because *every morning is not the same.*

I may need to do something extra in the morning such as set the table for a dinner party I will give when I get home from work. But I've *planned* to do it the night before. Or if I'm going to get up in the morning and study for a speech, I think about that the night before and everything is laid out.

Morning is *the* most crucial time for any woman. My life is easier because I don't have anybody else in the household except for my dog, Jolly, to be taken care of, and it's still complicated by different things I might have to do. If you're a woman who has children and a husband and you must go to work and you get up in the morning without a plan, anything can go wrong—and usually does.

You'll leave the house feeling frazzled, tired, annoyed; not together, mentally or physically. In this condition, you're facing a hard day at work. No wonder we so frequently hear: "I never should have gotten up this morning—everything's gone wrong!"

If the day starts off wrong, it's likely to continue in the same vein; if it starts off smoothly, everything else seems to fall into place, too.

Many women I have come in contact with and many in the Gillette study maintain they have a morning routine, but still find the a.m. hours hectic:

"My mornings are crazy, hectic, rushed," says one woman. "I normally get up about six. I straighten up whatever has to be straightened up, get to the shower and take care of myself, wake my daughter, dress her, make breakfast, spend a little time with her, then take her to nursery school and get to my office in time so I can sit and read the paper. It's always very hectic. In fact, my daughter said to my sitter the other morning, '*We run all morning.*'"

When asked what her biggest time-waster in the morning was, this woman replied: "I don't think there's any waste that I could eliminate. It's all things I have to do . . . I don't have a plan— I have a routine."

The problem with a routine is that we become so accustomed to it that we never stop to think there might be a better way. By accepting her routine as normal, this woman accepts everything she is currently doing as essential. If she were to stop and ask herself "What would happen if I don't get these toys picked up or what will happen if I don't do these dishes *now*, but wait till after work?" her mornings might flow a little easier, leave her with more energy to get things accomplished when she gets home.

## WHY MAKE THAT BED?

Admittedly, there is a morning problem. My mother always told me to make my bed before I left the house, and it was years before I could convince myself that *nothing* would happen if I left the house, bed unmade.

Habit and aesthetics tell us everything should be in order before we close the door; logic tells us that dirty dishes are a small price to pay for a smoothly running morning, hence a smooth day. Shouldn't we choose logic over habit?

Priorities for the morning are as useful as for the rest of your life. If bed making is a priority for you, fine. But it shouldn't become a priority until you've really evaluated that time (with the time log); seen what your time-wasters are; and decided very deliberately what absolutely has to be done before leaving the house:

You *must* get dressed.

The children most likely must be fed (but *must* they have bacon and eggs every morning?)

*Must* the dishes be washed or the living room vacuumed?

Not surprisingly, the women in the Gillette study disliked whatever takes most time. Perhaps a little more surprisingly, more working women without children mentioned disliking personal grooming; working women with children disliked meal preparation and household chores.

Also not surprisingly, the women chose the most relaxing activities as most liked (having coffee or tea, reading the paper or reading while listening to the radio, and showering).

If we apply the "What will happen if . . ." question to these relaxing activities (e.g., What will happen if I read? Nothing, except my children may go hungry), time for you in the morning would logically be first to go. It always is, isn't it?

Yet women who manage to find time for themselves during these busy hours find it so beneficial to the remainder of the day that this could be a crucial 15 or 45 minutes to work into your morning.

"I'm a morning person," says newspaper editor Harriet Simpson. "I get up about an hour earlier than I really need to because I think better and do better in the morning. A lot of the time I'll do some planning then. I seem to have a higher energy level in the morning and many times I'll do the supper dishes in the morning, gather up the laundry—simple things, not basic cleaning."

For Simpson, this hour constitutes practically the only time for herself.

Gail Buchalter (free-lance writer): "Mornings are my prime time. I get up early, about 6:30, which I've done since I've had a child. Then we have breakfast together—I have coffee, he has breakfast. Some mornings we talk and some mornings we watch cartoons. Then I take him to school, I jog, I come back home, and I either get down to work or I lose the day."

## WHAT CAN YOU SKIP?

For those of us who absolutely can't get up any earlier than we do already, we might try instead to eliminate some of what we're doing now and create a few minutes to relax by ourselves or at least to make everything else run a little more smoothly (which in itself will prove to be relaxing in the long run).

No law says household chores need to be done in the morning. Take a look at what you're doing now and see if there's anything you can eliminate.

Check your morning route closely. If it resembles the zigzag course I described at the beginning of the chapter, you could really use a strategy. *Complete all activities in a particular room before moving to another.* All the movement from bedroom-to-bathroom-to-kitchen-to-bedroom-etc. takes a lot of unnecessary energy and time.

## FORGET THE EGGS

While the family breakfast can be quality time well spent, it won't be if you insist on making bacon and eggs every morning. The cooking and cleanup take tremendous time and keep you away from the table, away from the rest of the family.

Many nutritious convenience foods are now on the market, and convenience is just what you need in the morning. Don't feel you're neglecting your duty if you use such foods.

Household chores that you cannot eliminate can at least be simplified. Use appliances, services, and products that will do the job in the fastest way. And ask your children and husband to help whenever necessary. All can make their own beds. Children can clear the breakfast table. Husband can do the dishes from the night before.

## COMBING HAIR IN THE CAR: WHO NEEDS IT?

When we asked Rosalie Davies, a musician and librarian, about her morning planning, she laughed: "Morning planning! I don't have any! All I do is leap out of bed and try to get into the car on time to get to work. I do all kinds of things when I'm in the car—comb my hair, put on my makeup —and I usually eat in the car. Usually I have my clothes planned, but I have to press them in the morning."

"Why?" we asked.

"I don't know, I guess I must leave the worst till the last."

While Davies laughs about her "worst mornings," she's looking for ways to improve them. Linda Koe, who studied time management, made the effort to improve and says:

"At one point, mornings were absolutely horrible for me. Now morning is one of my absolutely best times. I've cleared away everything that's nonessential to me getting to work, and that's all I have to do in the morning. My children are at an age (11 and 13) where they can do a lot of things for themselves. They'll get themselves ready for school in the morning; they feed themselves. I make sure there's milk and juice and cereal and toast. They clean up the kitchen when they're done. They take care of the dog in the morning. My husband takes care of himself, out of total neglect on my part." She laughs. "So all I have to do is get myself ready."

Before she streamlined her mornings, Koe "would get out the crockpot and get things started for dinner; start a load of laundry; supervise the things going on in the kitchen, making sure that everybody sat down and ate—I didn't always do it all, but I was in control, orchestrating the whole thing."

## SPOT YOUR PEAKS AND VALLEYS

Everybody has peak periods, and morning is one time when such peaks (or valleys) become most obvious: You may be a highly energized person like Harriet Simpson or you may be a zombie like Diana Silcox. Whichever you are, you must still perform an abnormal number of functions in an absurdly limited time period.

Three basic ways can make mornings less hectic, which will result in a less hectic day:

*Get up earlier:* Whether you give yourself an extra hour or just 15 minutes, the time can be used to relax, plan, do chores (if you must). Any extra time seems like a gift, so you might try alloting these 15 more minutes a day until it seems easy.

*Simplify:* Some people just can't get up any earlier. The time in bed is time for *them*. If that's you, try to make your mornings less hectic by eliminating chores (bed making) and/or getting help in those chores you must do and/or using more time-saving devices and services.

*Plan:* If you can neither get up early nor eliminate chores, planning is essential. The night before, prepare everything you'll need the next day: wardrobe, papers for work, lunches and money for children, breakfasts, even your to-do list. Though you may still be a morning zombie, you'll find that things can run smoothly, leaving you time to react to the unexpected. Check with your family for their needs.

Despite best efforts, things will not always run smoothly. There will always be crises—that's what life's about. I've even gotten caught in the morning, and I plan *everything*.

I always prepare my clothes the night before. Once I picked up my clothes from the cleaner and was going to wear the blouse to a very important meeting I had that morning. I had the suit laid out, my handbag, briefcase, shoes. Everything was "perfect."

Next morning I got up a little later than usual. I thought it was OK because everything was ready. It would just take a few minutes to hop into the shower and get myself together. No panic. Then I put the blouse on. Two buttons had been lost at the cleaner's. I had not checked the blouse. I'd just assumed it would be fine. Now I didn't have time to sew on new buttons, much less look for a matching pair.

So I had to find something else to wear, which may sound simple enough, but remember I'm one of those morning zombies. For me it was a crisis, particularly since I had overslept.

Anybody can get caught, despite planning. Routine planning does, however, make such crises happen less often, and seem less critical when they do happen since everything else is presumably running according to plan.

*People ask me if I don't think I'm ridiculous planning everything out. I say that there are enough things that can go wrong without me compounding it by not having essential things planned.*

# THE SUPERCOORDINATED WARDROBE

Planning your wardrobe isn't where good planning stops, but it's crucial to women who run around in the morning and then must go to work looking cool and professional. Some women plan their entire wardrobe so everything in the closet is coordinated. Even zombies can reach into the closet, pull out a blouse, a jacket, and a skirt, and two hours later when they're fully awake, find the outfit is coordinated.

This canny idea is catching on as more and more working women find less and less time to shop, and embark on only a few but all-encompassing trips to the stores that enable them to coordinate the entire season's or even year's wardrobe.

The time-saving is twofold: You save time shopping *and* you save time in the future by not having to stop to worry about what blouse goes with what skirt and if the blouse you need is clean. Since everything within a set of clothes matches everything else, the coast is clear, provided you take care of your clothes as

# IS TIME ON YOUR SIDE IN THE MORNING?

How effectively are you managing your morning? Don't guess. Take this quiz and really find out. Rate yourself by choosing the description that fits you best.

1. I manage my morning time by preparing a to-do list which gives me a plan for each day's morning routine.

a. ☐ Always
b. ☐ Sometimes          Score_____
c. ☐ Never

2. I establish priorities each morning, and concentrate on accomplishing only those activities which are *most* important to me and/or my family.

a. ☐ Always
b. ☐ Sometimes          Score_____
c. ☐ Never

3. Time is money and I save extra time by investing in products and/or services that decrease my personal time involvement.

a. ☐ Always
b. ☐ Sometimes          Score_____
c. ☐ Never

6. Breakfast is the most important meal of the day. I prepare breakfast every morning for me and/or my family, and cooking time takes:

a. ☐ 15 minutes or less
b. ☐ Between 15 and 20 minutes
                        Score_____
c. ☐ More than 20 minutes

7. I know I can't accomplish everything in the morning so I delegate household responsibilities to my husband/children/roommate/outside help.

a. ☐ Always
b. ☐ Sometimes          Score_____
c. ☐ Never

8. I like to experiment with different hairstyles and makeup techniques in the morning.

a. ☐ Never
b. ☐ Sometimes          Score_____
c. ☐ Always

## Scoring

Give yourself

10 points for each (a) answer
5 points for each (b) answer
-2 points for each (c) answer

## Rating

Below 40   Time is definitely not on your side! You're letting it run away from you. It's time to take the *mis-* out of managing your morning.

40–60      Accent should be on what you *must* do. Eliminate chores that you can't get through.

61–80      Got to admit you're getting better—but there are still steps to take to beat the clock.

4. I spend a lot of time in the morning doing a little bit of everything and moving from room to room (bedroom-to-bathroom-to-kitchen-to-bathroom, etc.).

a. ☐ Never (I complete all activities in one room before moving to the next)

b. ☐ Sometimes          Score _____

c. ☐ Always

5. Every morning brings another unexpected "crisis." It ranges from no clean underwear, to "My stockings all have runs," to "There's no toilet paper," to "The coffee has run out."

a. ☐ Infrequently

b. ☐ The unexpected occurs once a week          Score _____

c. ☐ The unexpected occurs two or more times every week

9. I can never decide what to wear in the morning, so I try on several outfits to find what fits my mood.

a. ☐ Never

b. ☐ Sometimes          Score _____

c. ☐ Always

10. I make sure that I have time for personal activities, i.e., exercising, reading, or even thinking in the morning.

a. ☐ Always

b. ☐ Sometimes          Score _____

c. ☐ Never

81–100     You're an effective time manager. Keep up the good work and you'll continue to reap the benefits.

Remember, getting the most from your time means developing priorities, allocating time for specific tasks, simplifying activities, and taking advantage of time-saving products and services.

Why don't you try it? It may just give you the "time of your life"!

you take them off at night—dirty clothes in hamper, a special box for dry cleaning, clean clothes put away.

The same strategy can work for children's and husband's clothes: Keep them basic and coordinated and your mornings will be a lot easier; husbands stop yelling for matching socks and children stop emerging fully dressed in hopelessly mismatched outfits.

*Mornings are a microcosm of the day.* Keeping that in mind, apply the specific time management principles we've already discussed to your mornings and they'll be just as well controlled, with flexibility for those things you can't control, as the rest of your life. And do try the quiz on pages 230–31.

# *Home Tips*

---

ALTHOUGH time management ranks *effectiveness* over *efficiency,* it certainly doesn't exclude efficiency. Obviously, efficiency is going to save time; five minutes here and another three there. Since time is cumulative, good organization helps you to accumulate it.

We've collected specific time-saving tips that represent the best of thousands we've heard about and used ourselves. While they'll ease *doing* what you can't avoid doing forever, they're not substitutes for the time management principles we've already presented.

Maybe you've heard of the woman who, having decided that when the first day of school came around *this* year she would not be caught unawares, made every effort to get things organized on time: it worked so well that she brought her child to school a day too early!

The moral is: *Overdoing is always harmful, even when it comes to efficiency.*

Organization is only efficient when it goes hand in hand with effectiveness. So whenever you can, doing *less* still is preferable to doing more quicker.

But when you just can't eliminate anything, the following tips are definitely time-savers.

# HOW TO SAVE GROOMING TIME

Plan and complete your personal grooming needs before the family gets up. This is the time to devote to yourself.

Stagger the bathroom schedule so there is no unnecessary morning crush.

No time and place for exercise? Try exercising while bathing. Seriously! It works. Always place a rubber mat or rubber strips on the floor of your shower or tub for safe footing.

Try shaving underarms and legs in the evening. If you must shave in the morning, do it in the shower. Also, slot the real time-consuming grooming tasks (depilation or bleaching, nail polishing, eyebrow plucking, etc.) for the night.

If others have to use your bathroom, make a room elsewhere in the house (with good lighting) to put on makeup and fix hair. Also, keep all of your makeup supplies in one place. The plastic organizer tray with multisized compartments works extremely well. Should someone else need the mirror, you can easily pick up the tray and move to another room.

Ask a cosmetician about products and techniques to apply makeup in the fastest way. Tell her your morning time is limited, but you still want to look your best. All-purpose beauty coloring crayons, for example, make morning makeup the quickest yet. They can be used on your eyes, brows, cheeks, and lips.

Karen Olson puts her makeup on *before* showering. According to experts, this gives your face a soft glow.

You might consider using less makeup. Heresy? To some. But do ask yourself if you really *need* all the makeup you're currently wearing.

Consult your hairdresser about the easiest, fastest hair-care method for your type of hair. If your hair requires daily setting, try electric rollers or a curling iron. These appliances can save you time and/or you can accomplish another chore simultaneously.

Set your hair before showering; the steam will set the hair and it'll dry while you dress.

Permanents may be expensive, but they save time and cut down on future haircuts in the long run. Also, short hair is not only fashionable, it's easy to care for.

On the weekend, organize your clothes for each day of the coming week. Put your complete outfit on one hanger if possible. If not, use wire fasteners to hold the hangers together. Attach a plastic bag containing underwear, stockings, and accessories to the hanger. Plan the children's wardrobe the same way. Preplanning will immediately identify that articles of clothing need to be washed, ironed, or repaired. If preplanning is a problem, always decide the night before what you'll wear. Spontaneous decisions in the morning are wonderful luxuries; too bad most working women can't afford them.

Invest in an all-week purse, one that coordinates with every outfit you own. It's sheer chaos to switch handbags midweek.

## HOW TO SAVE TIME ON FOOD PREPARATION

When you make breakfast, remember: *Keep it simple.* The more cooking, the more cleanup time.

Simple to prepare (yet well-balanced) breakfasts:

1. *The blender breakfast:* one egg, one small banana, orange juice, wheat germ and honey.
2. *Instant breakfast mix.*
3. *Instant hot cereal with fruit.*
4. *The toaster breakfast:* pop tarts, frozen waffles, Danish, muffins; add a glass of juice and coffee.

5. *Egg and fruit breakfast:* A hard-boiled egg (cooked the night before) with a piece of fruit is not only low in calories, but also a quick, nutritious meal.

Use "convenience" foods without guilt: conveniently stored, conveniently prepared, conveniently cleaned up.

When you plan dinner, consider: What can be used for future lunches? Make sandwiches and store in the freezer. If you pack lunches daily, set out boxes or bags the night before and pack non-perishables (cookies, fruit, pretzels). Add sandwiches from the freezer in the morning; they'll thaw by noon.

Cook quantities that leave enough leftovers to freeze for future dinners. Turkeys and large roasts notoriously (but helpfully) leave plenty of leftovers for the week. Casseroles, spaghetti sauces, vegetables—nearly everything freezes well, and if you double or triple the recipe, you'll find you're cutting future cooking time immensely.

A design study has shown that opening and shutting cupboard doors is one of our invisible time-wasters. When possible, keep all utensils (and sometimes food) in open storage situations; it makes access quicker. (Petty? Don't kid yourself! It all adds up.)

Allow yourself to eat out at fast-food places (hamburgers, fish, chicken, pizza, sandwiches) and occasionally at "real" restaurants—for you.

## HOW TO SAVE TIME ON HOUSEHOLD CHORES

Simplify bed making. Use a washable quilt or comforter; smooth the bottom sheet and comforter into place—the bed is made! Use the same principle for children's beds: the kids can do it themselves.

Keep a sponge under the soap in the bathroom. You'll never have to deal with a messy soap dish and you'll always have a sponge handy for wiping the sink.

Everyone over the age of five is, theoretically, capable of cleaning a tub and sink. Unless there's a major grime buildup, most tubs and sinks come clean with a soapy sponge.

Major grime buildup in the tub? Clean it *during* your shower. Bring the cleanser into the shower with you, and scrub as you finish washing. This saves time and also does away with the back-bending contortions of trying to scrub a tub from the outside. And when you're finished cleaning the tub, you can wash the cleanser off yourself immediately!

While emptying the dishwasher or drainer, set the table for the next meal.

When you must vacuum, dust, etc., pick one room per morning. Better to completely clean up one room than have all rooms partly cleaned.

Use the washing machine as a hamper for white clothes. Tell the family all white laundry goes into the machine immediately. No presorting, and you can wash a load when the machine is full.

Load dishwasher after each meal, but only wash dishes once a day.

Schedule your errands (dry cleaning, shoe repair, laundry) for one day a week so that one family member, not always you, can become responsible for everything. Separate boxes for things that need doing (dry cleaning, soleless shoes, etc.) signal the responsibility of each family member to keep track of his own needs.

If space allows, organize an out-in-the open system for outerwear (raincoats, boots, hats) so in the morning crush everybody finds what's needed. The arrangement also makes it more inviting to people, children included, to put things away, since "away" is merely hanging clothes on an easily accessible hook.

*Long-run tips:*

Betty Harragan (author of *Games Mother Never Taught You*): "Housecleaning in general is a waste of time. That's why I don't accumulate things that I don't have time to maintain. My idea of furniture is to buy stuff that will almost last forever; buy the kind that requires the utter, absolute least maintenance."

Jenita Cargile (confidential investigator): "About every three months I go through closets and shelves and throw away everything we don't need. I don't like to do it, but it makes everything neater and easier to take care of. You have to train yourself to say 'OK, I haven't worn that for a year, so what am I keeping it for?' "

## HOW TO SAVE TIME ON CHILD RELATED ACTIVITIES

Keep cleanup items—napkins, towels, glasses, etc.—at a convenient level for children to reach.

It's hard for children to fold towels neatly, but they can put them through rings. When buying towel rings, get the self-stick kind and place them at the child's level.

Cleanup should be a family affair. Little children can carry dirty cups and plates to the sink; older children can put dishes in the dishwasher.

Eliminate the early morning search for small change for milk money, transportation, etc., by marking an envelope with each child's name and attaching the envelopes to the refrigerator door with a magnet. That way the child can check the refrigerator each day before leaving for school and pick up his money.

The refrigerator door is also a great place for leaving messages and to-do lists for other family members.

Taking children to school or nursery is an ideal time to be alone with them and talk about their feelings and needs. While this may not be possible every day, positioning "Tuesday morning is our time," can be exciting and something to look forward to.

Put a paper cup dispenser near the refrigerator and have at least one refrigerator shelf stocked with items you want to make accessible to children—milk, healthy snacks, etc. And try to set one table or counter low enough for a child to reach comfortably.

## HOW TO BUY TIME

Gadgets are designed to save time, yet every gadget may not be right for you. Some merely restructure time, which is a help; others actually shorten the time it takes to do something. Here's a list of gadgets that may be ideal for you:

*Crock pot:* The typical time restructurer. It takes the usual time for a one-pot meal, but you can do it the night before or in the morning and go to work or sneak off to the beach and come home to a completely cooked dinner. Caution: The time it takes to clean a crock pot can often negate its convenience.

*Dishwasher:* Especially good for larger families. Singles and couples may find it more energy-wasting than time-efficient. Weigh your own needs carefully.

*Microwave oven:* Designed with the working woman in mind, these ovens are becoming more intricate. A study has shown that more people use microwave ovens for boiling water than anything else. But that saves time too!

*Blender:* Great for blender breakfasts and simple chopping and pureeing. Again, blenders have evolved into intricate creatures.

*Food processor:* If you do a lot of cooking, this may be the ideal time-saver, with the cost being well worth it. Combining the functions of blender and mixer, the processor also slices, chops, grinds—everything, as some wit put it, except walk the dog. Maybe next year!

*Cassette tape recorder:* Fighting off my morning zombie state, I use the recorder while I get ready for work. I practice speeches or dictate ideas or thoughts for later in the day. Here are some of this gadget's infinite uses:

Record a message to children for all instructions they need when returning from school. It's so much nicer to hear a tape in mom's own voice.

Many new books and all the classics are on cassette tapes. Listen to a book while doing something else.

Record any lectures and classes you attend; then study while you fix your hair or pedal your exercise bike.

Exercise classes have been put on tape. You can now have individual instruction whenever you want—and you can take the instructor with you on trips!

Jenita Cargile uses her two hours a day commuting time to learn new languages with her tape recorder. Other courses are also available in this format. You can't read while driving, but you can certainly listen.

*Beeper:* Tone-only or tone-and-voice units enable you to remain in constant touch with family members and co-workers, relieving you of the necessity of being near phones at prearranged times. Another good investment to save future time.

## SERVICES THAT SAVE TIME

Buy time by paying for services that will free your own time:

*Housekeeper:* The $30 or so per week that this costs buys you an entire Saturday or weekend to spend with husband and children.

## Home Tips

*Part-time helper:* Ask a baby-sitter to do a load of laundry; hire a neighborhood teenager to do specific cleaning chores; pay your children to do some chores that you feel may be above and beyond routine delegation.

*Laundry:* Not only dry-cleaning services, but also daily laundry. Such services are usually surprisingly inexpensive.

*Lawn care:* If you don't like to do the yard, pay someone to do it. Neighborhood youngsters don't charge exorbitant rates for adequate service.

*Baby-sitters:* Paying a baby-sitter for an evening out is a relatively small price to pay for your mental health.

*Shopping:* Ask a friend who likes to grocery-shop if she'll do yours, either for extra money or for an exchange of services. Five dollars may go a long way in inspiring the teenager next door to shop from your list. A master list such as our example can save you even more time. Make several copies and just check the depleted items *as* you notice they're needed. Recognizing the fact that working women have little time to shop, wardrobe services are cropping up everywhere. They range from the personalized all-in-one-boutique (where you can quickly outfit yourself completely) to the professional shopper who acts as sort of an interior decorator to your body and shops for you! Everything costs a little more, but the cost may be worth it. Use delivery services whenever offered. Many food stores are open on weekends and late in the evenings (some 24 hours). Shopping at 10:00 p.m. or even 2:00 a.m. may be the best time for you—and you don't have to fret on line at the checkout counter.

*Mail order:* Responding to the energy crisis and the working woman's pressures, more and more businesses are opening mail-order departments. Many encourage shopping by phone. The old standbys (L. L. Bean, Sears, J. C. Penney) are still among the best; the last two are particularly good for children's clothes and housewares. Until recently, most mail-order houses specialized in gifts, but that's all changed. The best way to locate mail-order

# SHOPPING LIST

### DAIRY
milk
butter
margarine
eggs
yogurt
sour-cream
cream cheese
cheddar
Swiss
Parmesan
Ricotta
Boursin

### MEAT
chicken
beef
veal
pork
stewing meat
sausage
hot dogs
chopped meat
ham
bacon
cutlets
roasts
chops
fish

### FROZEN
corn
broccoli
string beans
brussels sprouts
asparagus
mixed vegetables
ice cream
pie crust
sherbet
orange juice
apple juice
grape juice
grapefruit juice
lemonade
iced tea

### PERSONAL
toothpaste
dental floss
shaving cream
razor blades
cream rinse
shampoo
mouthwash
nail file
deodorant

### SOUPS
instant
canned
box

### BREAD
white
rye
whole wheat
protein
pumpernickel
bagels
corn muffin
English muffins
dinner rolls
salad croutons
bread crumbs

### DRY GOODS
cereal
coffee
tea
rice
beans
sugar
flour
powdered milk
pancake mix
cake mix
macaroni
potato chips
hot chocolate
crackers

### LIQUOR
### WINE
### BEER

### PRODUCE
lettuce
tomatoes
onions
cucumbers
peppers
potatoes
yams
carrots
garlic cloves
celery
fruit

### CONDIMENTS
oil
vinegar
ketchup
mustard
relish
salad dressing

### SPICES
salt
pepper
basil
oregano
garlic powder
cinnamon
allspice
sage

### PAPER GOODS
toilet paper
facial tissues
napkins
paper towels
lunch bags
garbage bags
waxed paper
aluminum foil

### CANNED GOODS
applesauce
peas
pork and beans
sauerkraut
jelly
peanut butter
mayonnaise
tuna fish
tomato juice
condensed milk
spaghetti sauce

### OTHER
_____
_____
_____
_____
_____

### HOUSEHOLD
bath soap
dish detergent
laundry detergent
bleach
spray cleaner
cleanser
soap pads
light bulbs
oven cleaner
ammonia
toilet cleaner
deodorizer

### CONFECTIONS
candy
peanuts
raisins
brownie mix
powdered sugar
chocolate chips

sources is the back pages of magazines. Use some of your waiting time (in offices, etc.) to wander through these pages for sources that will save *you* time.

*Credit cards* can save time shopping by phone. Department stores and boutiques with catalogs often permit you to charge your purchases, saving the time it would take to validate a personal check. Shopping by credit card also provides you with a detailed receipt, a time-saver for tax purposes. Credit cards can be used to reserve tickets for plays, concerts, planes (have the airline mail tickets and avoid standing on long airport lines!), hotel rooms, sending flowers.


## THE SUPERSERVICE APARTMENT

Hotel sales manager Donna Davis of Dallas makes use of what has got to be the ultimate time-saver for working women (although it's aimed at the elderly): the full-service apartment.

"It's a 22-story high rise, close to downtown, a mile from my hotel, which is very convenient. Amenities of the condominium include people who park the car and also service and wash the car when needed. We have a house phone to call down for the car as well. When we have guests, the doormen can call up to us to tell us who's there if we haven't left word we're expecting someone (great to guard against drop-in visitors!). We have 24-hour security surveillance. There's maid service. They'll walk my dog if I'm out of town and they'll water the plants. We have a little restaurant and can have room service.

"I hate housework. I have a little sign that says 'To hell with housework.' I'd rather be doing something else than vacuuming or dusting. I don't mind paying for services. If I've got a Saturday or a Sunday off, I don't want to spend it cleaning my house or taking my car to the shop to have it worked on or washing it. They do that. It's wonderful!"

When you buy time, it's as shrewd an investment to get an extra-long telephone cord as it is to pay extra for services. Learn to put a price on your time; then determine what services or gadgets are worth the price.

## RECOMMENDED READING FOR MORE TIME-SAVERS

The above are only samples of available time-saving tips. Another book could be written on such specifics—and several already have been. Three of the best:

*Mary Ellen's Best of Helpful Hints* by Mary Ellen Pinkham and Pearl Higginbotham (Warner/B. Lansky Books). One of the problems with tips is we can never find them when we need them. This compact spiral-bound collection solves that problem and all hints are pretested for you.

*Getting Organized* by Stephanie Winston (W. W. Norton). She offers very simple ways to put your life in order, from closets to budget.

*Superwoman* by Shirley Conran (Crown Publishers). We overlooked the odious implication of the title to peruse Conran's book, which includes great tips on everything "for every woman who hates housework"—from preserving foods to preserving self.

In addition to these books, two magazines that continually provide excellent time-saving tips and advice to working women are *Working Woman* magazine and *Working Mother* (published by McCall's). Both are invaluable aids to working women, and make eye-opening "waiting-time" reading material.

One of the most amusing tips we stumbled over came from

Jackie Friss, who admits she sometimes writes something down on a calendar and then forgets to look at the calendar!

"Let me tell you something that I found to be absolutely great, and it really works. When my neighbors did this, we all used to laugh at them. As you walked into their house there was a short hallway and there were pieces of paper on the floor. I used to wonder: 'What's this paper on the floor?' They'd say, 'Those are notes.' I'd say, 'What are they doing here?' And they'd say, 'Well, it doesn't work writing them on calendars or the bulletin board, so now we put them in the doorway so we step on them.'

"And you know? Every so often if we have a dentist appointment or something, and I know we'll never look at the calendar to remember it, I drop a note right in the middle of the floor. As I go out to work in the morning, I step on the piece of paper and I know that something is coming up that day. I wish I had written myself a note that you were going to call tonight!"

# TV or Not TV?

TELEVISION can certainly be a prime-time time-waster; but only if we let it.

I've already mentioned my penchant for game shows, which I watch when I know I have time and simply want to relax.

Television is a terrific example of what time management is all about: *When we control the times we watch TV, rather than letting the TV control us* we're applying good time management to a very specific part of our lives.

If we follow the advice of other time management experts who advocate getting rid of the family set, we're admitting to ourselves that we're not capable of controlling our habits. As I've said, It's a theory I totally disagree with. Keep your set—but do learn to be aware of how much time you're spending in front of it instead of doing something you'd rather be doing. Figure it yourself:

An episode of "Mork and Mindy" could be a leisurely soak in the tub, a chance to pay some bills, the 30 minutes you need to begin exercising.

A marathon night with "Charlie's Angels" and "Vegas" could have been spent on a German course or taking your children to a movie or for ice cream . . .

If you feel that what you needed for that 30 minutes or that two hours was the time to simply zonk out in front of the set, then that's time well spent as long as you realize what you're doing. The major criticism of television is that we watch it *without being aware* of the time we're wasting. That's not merely a time-waster; that's a real killer.

Commercial banking representative Linda Koe expresses universal mixed feelings about television: "There are times when I want total escape and that's when I sit down and zonk out in front of the TV. I realized that even though I didn't like it, I was watching more of it than I wanted to, and if I would stop doing that I'd have time to do the other things. Television is one of the biggest time-wasters there ever was. At one point we were actually going to go cold turkey and have no television, but I realized there are some programs I do want to see.

"It's the way we use TV. I get real upset when I hear people say 'Oh, my life would be great if we didn't have television; my family used to talk at mealtime and now they just sit and watch TV'—like it's the TV's fault! I say, 'Wait a minute, who made the decision to turn the darn thing on?' "

Koe's recognition of TV's time-wasting seductiveness enabled her to break away from its hypnotic effects without cold turkey withdrawal pains.

Like many women, she finds TV can be a center for family togetherness, and she'll frequently bring her weights to the set and lift them while the children watch. There are some excellent shows on TV—Koe cited Baryshnikov at the White House—which do make great ways to spend "family time" while enjoying, learning, and discussing during and after.

Television may be sealing its own doom. Ratings indicate that viewing is on the decline. People are either not happy with what's being televised or simply do not have the time to waste watching television—and perhaps have finally recognized they do not have that time.

Judy Sommerschield, owner of Schield Personnel, told us: "I don't watch a lot of TV. I *try* sometimes. There was one week when every night I wanted to come home and watch TV and every night I'd look at the *TV Guide* and there was not even one thing I could convince myself that I could've even wanted to sit down and watch—and I'll watch almost anything."

The paucity of good viewing, coupled with our growing awareness of time, has taken television from the dark recesses of "subconscious" time-waster and put it in the spotlight where it belongs.

So when it comes to fighting television time-wasting, remember the best ways to control it:

1. Recognize whether watching is your priority at the moment (would you really rather be doing something else?).

2. If you'd rather be doing something else, remember what the OFF button is for—and press it.

# Home, Sweet Office

I have an office. I tried working out of my home once and there were just a lot of negative factors about it.

—GENEVIEVE MEEK
*Free-lance illustrator*

I'd probably hate going to an office every day. What I'm looking for is a loosely controlled life that's geared to functioning without a lot of regimentation.

—GAIL BUCHALTER
*Free-lance writer*

MANY WOMEN have time problems that have nothing to do with getting up in the morning, getting to the office on time, getting home in time to fix a good dinner. These are the growing number of women who work out of their homes, maybe because they're in a free-lance occupation or, as was once my case, beginning their own business and avoiding the overhead of an office.

Their time problem is, paradoxically, an asset that women who do go to work profess to envy: "All that *unstructured time*—what I wouldn't give for that!"

Unstructured time comes with as many pitfalls as the "normal" structure (morning time, an eight-hour office day, drive time, dinnertime, TV time, bedtime). Let's check out the disadvantages and advantages of working out of your home. Some people thrive on it; others cannot do it or hate it.

Self-discipline is one obvious key. When I started my business out of my apartment, I created my own structured time system to establish my own discipline. It worked very effectively. I set my workday to run from 9:00 a.m. to 5:00 p.m., with some overtime permitted (the one flaw!). I would dress fully, as though going to an office, and be at my desk by 9:00 a.m. I stayed at the desk (my entire office area) until lunchtime, when I'd either take a break and have lunch at the park (to get out of the apartment), or would have lunch for one-hour and be back at my desk where I would work until "closing" time.

The plan worked for me because—maybe you've noticed—I am very disciplined, a vast blessing. I set up my goals beforehand, so I *knew* I wanted to work at home and what I would have to do to make it work.

The advantages to this arrangement are obvious.

*Low overhead:* Although business advisers advocate beginning your own business with some capital—usually an intimidating amount—many women plunge into the entrepreneurial world with high hopes and low cash reserves. It's great not to have to spend what cash you do have or earn on a high-rent office. I put my money to work at things I considered more important until I could afford a business office. When I could, I did. I also wanted to work in my home, but I moved because the business grew so quickly that it required more space than my apartment offered.

*If you have small children, child care is easier:* Gail Buchalter's son is in a preschool with flexibility. "He's in for full days," says Buchalter, "but I pick him up early on the days that I can. And I take him in a little bit later on mornings that I can. I was told by the school, which kind of relieved my mind, that they thought it was better to leave him in for five days and shorten them whenever possible than to put him in for three or four full days. So I did what fit in with my life."

*You can choose your working hours:* Here's where "unstructured" time is a blessing. Sleeping late is a privilege of those who don't have a clock to punch, figuratively or literally. At the end of the day, you can make up for that luxury by working later than five.

## MAKING YOUR OWN HOURS

Choosing your own working hours can become a severe handicap. When we don't face time in prefabricated *blocks*, as we do when we must be at work at a certain time, take a certain hour for lunch and so forth, we may be overwhelmed by the infinite choices of an amorphous 24-hour day and frequently mislead ourselves into thinking we have more time than we actually do.

If you're considering working out of your home, you must be extremely frank with yourself and ask: *"Am I disciplined enough to work at home? Am I capable of shutting out the distractions inevitable in a home office environment or incorporating those distractions into my workday?"*

Gail Buchalter, the free-lance writer, uses the "distractions" as an advantage: "I clean all through the day. That's one nice thing about working at home and writing; when I get stuck for an idea, I'll get up and dust while I think, or vacuum or do the floors."

While some women can successfully combine the nonrelated aspects of working at home with their careers, others find housework totally distracting or, more insidious, a form of procrastination. The temptation is undeniable. On unpressured days it may be easier to do the dishes than work toward your goals. Friends tend to think that your being home means you're available for socializing. They'll drop in and you must know how to convince them you're working.

More important, you must be able to convince *yourself* you're working!

## YOUR OFFICE AT HOME

Set up a work area that's all yours. Working at a dining-room table only to have to clear it off each night to eat dinner will prove frustrating, not to mention time-wasting. If you cannot arrange to have a separate room, portion off an area, complete with telephone and any files, drawing boards, or other equipment and papers necessary to your job. This work space should be used only for your work and only this space should be used to work.

This professional "office area" will reflect a serious attitude on your part and will go a long way toward dispelling one of the problems Genevieve Meek, the illustrator, encountered when she worked at home: "There were some problems about my being taken really seriously. Some people tended to think I was working for pin money." Meek also "missed the daily interaction of coming into a place—getting dressed, combing my hair, and going out and meeting people."

And she faced another problem inherent in working at home: *working too much.* "I couldn't really divorce myself from work long enough to do anything else. When it comes down to a choice between putting in the wash or drawing, I'll take drawing any time."

## IT'S HARD TO QUIT

While we tend to think that someone working at home can take time off whenever she wants, not taking time off is frequently a problem. Since the office is always there, we never actually leave it. "Just five more minutes" or "I think I'll catch up on some work tonight" are easy traps to fall into when it's so physically feasible—no long treks or drives to a downtown office.

Also, people who know you work at home may postpone making a call to you until late in the day or the evening, knowing they can always reach you. This can throw you into the permanent pressure cooker of a 24-hour workday unless you apply stern tactics. If you begin to get many evening and weekend business calls, you should not hesitate to tell callers what your "office hours" are. If you respect their personal time, they can bloody well respect yours.

Just as you must discipline yourself to work at home, you must discipline yourself to *not* work at home. Learn to close a mental door on your work or you'll find yourself working nights and weekends, as I did for too long (but no more).

What about the useful variety of meetings? Since most of us do not live in the hub of the business world, we must travel to meetings or interviews that mean something to us. Plan out-of-the-house meetings so that as many as possible fall on the same day; this leaves other days free for uninterrupted blocks of time. Gail Buchalter carries this one step further: She schedules her meetings and interviews for times that will enable her to drive clear of Los Angeles's infamous rush-hour traffic.

If there's no support staff (secretary or assistant) and no money for helpers you must play several "business roles"; I found this plays havoc with your time unless you discipline yourself. Originally, I turned to the easier "file-clerk" and "secretarial" jobs. When I found I wasn't accomplishing as much as I had intended, I took a new tack and set certain hours aside to be "secretary," certain hours to be "Diana Silcox, office consultant," and so forth. It worked beautifully for me.

Also helpful is an answering machine or service to screen out calls you can return at your convenience. And if you can afford part-time help, you'll free up time for you to concentrate on your major goals.

While some women work at home only until they can afford an office—e.g., myself—others work at home because they like it and find no need for an office—e.g., Gail Buchalter. Each person's habits and motivations are as different as her goals, so while one woman may turn to cleaning the tub to mull things over or relieve frustrations, another may use housecleaning as an excuse to put off a major work project.

The key is: *Woman, know thyself!* If you can work at home and incorporate the natural distractions into your workday or ignore them, the time benefits will be as great as they sound:

Uninterrupted blocks of time, even days, for major projects.

The potential for "playing hooky" and being good to yourself.

Avoiding commuting and other time-wasters common in office situations.

The ability to care for your children or be on call should you still decide to place them in a child-care situation.

## FRITTER, FRITTER, FRITTER

If you *aren't* disciplined and cannot stick to priorities, working at home can be catastrophic to your time:

You lose whole days without even knowing it.

You really do put off today what you can do tomorrow.

You fritter away valuable work time to do the dishes, vacuum the rug, clean the tub . . .

And since time is cumulative, those minutes can even cost you your business.

Buchalter has found the essential ingredient to successfully working at home: "I find that the more you do, the more there's time for. If I start out the day doing nothing, I'll continue to do nothing for the rest of the day. If I start out doing something, I'll add to it as I go along."

254

## Home, Sweet Office

While this is true in any situation, it's particularly applicable to working at home. Women who work at an office can always use the physical act of traveling to the office to give them a momentum for the rest of the day. Women who work at home must provide their own momentum. They must be self-starters.

Self-starting can be as simple as sitting at your desk and making your to-do list or making an exploratory phone call. Use it as the start of your "day at the office." No matter what your job is that enables you to work at home, make this *morning momentum* a daily habit and you won't be "losing the day" because you haven't gotten down to work.

# Time-Saving Tips for the Office

AN ORGANIZED OFFICE and work system will prevent wasting time that you may not be aware you're wasting.

Although your time log should pinpoint most of your problems, there are a few points you may not recognize because you're unaware of a more efficient way of getting something done. When you use them along with the *effective* time-savers (delegation, saying no, saying goodbye, communication, compromising on perfectionism, and so forth), the following efficiency-oriented tips will prove invaluable.

## HOW TO SAVE TIME ON PAPERWORK

All efficiency experts including myself know three things you can do with any piece of paper:

1. Throw it away.
2. Act on it.
3. File it.

To speed the flow of paperwork, whether it's the daily arrival of your mail or the stream of reports, schedules, etc., from co-workers, set up a system of file folders or baskets.

I use a five-tier basket, each with a specific designation:

1. In-box.
2. Out-box.
3. Meetings.
4. To-do.
5. Reading material.

When you open your mail from your in-box, each piece of paper either goes into the to-do tier if action is needed; or in the out-box if it must be filed or kept in follow-up (if so, your secretary should place this in a tickler file and remind you of the date it's due; also, mark the date in your calendar). Some incoming material you may want to go over later—magazines, articles, reports, courses, etc.; put this in your reading material tier so when you leave your office and want something to read on the bus or taxi (or to take when you're going somewhere and may be kept waiting) you can simply take something from the basket, eliminating the desperate last-minute search for an article "I know is here *somewhere*."


## THROW IT OUT!

When the reading material tier gets too full, plan a block of time to review its contents. Much is probably unimportant and can be thrown out. If there is a course you want to take but want to read about first, mark the date of the course in your calendar and the date you need to sign up so it doesn't slip by; make it a priority to read the description before attending the course.

Any material that doesn't fall into the above categories goes into the garbage because it's junk mail or something you have no intention of keeping. (Three-quarters of the material that crosses most people's desks falls into that category.)

Whenever possible, do the "to-do" items immediately. For example, if you get a request that needs only a brief reply, answer it on the piece of correspondence, make a copy of it on your copier, and prepare it for mailing. Most correspondence does not require a formal letter. If you don't want to answer on the original letter, try using a three-part reply message form. The original and the second copy are sent to the person addressed; the third copy is kept for your records. When your correspondent answers, she returns the second copy so you both have a copy of your original request and her reply on one piece of paper. You both have saved time; neither of you dictated and typed a formal letter.

The tier marked "Meetings" is for material you receive which you know you'll need during the week for meetings you'll be attending. On the date of the meeting, you can easily find what you need to take with you.

Marie McDonald, who operates her own elevator company, offers a great tip for women who belong to many organizations. It can also be adapted to other situations. She purchased plastic carry cases with hinged tops and handles, file folder size. The cases are stackable, taking up little space on your desk. Keep your files for individual organizations in separate cases, and when you're ready to leave for one meeting, simply grab the appropriate case and you'll have all the material you need, once again eliminating the last-minute search. McDonald also uses one of the cases as a sample case.

I tried the tip after talking to her and found it so useful that I immediately went out and bought several for a friend. I've found them great for the problem of what to do with all the papers you have while working on a project, especially if you have more than one project going at once. I have one in each color, one box for each project. Now all the files are in one convenient place, within arm's reach. (These handy cases are available at stationery and dime stores and cost less than ten dollars apiece.)

## HOW TO SAVE TIME ON FILES

There are many books about filing, so I will touch on it only briefly.

*Filing should be a system of retrieval, not storage:* Items that you may never need again but feel compelled to save simply take up room in your filing system. Be selective.

*Keep your file system as simple as possible:* No fancy headings or infinite breakdowns of subjects. Keeping the retrieval idea in mind, you want to know where to look for something when you need it without wasting precious time trying to remember under which clever heading you filed something.

The way the files are set up depends to a great extent on how they're used. One company I worked with had a problem in the order department. The files were numerical by order number. Customers calling would give the name of the company. Often the customers would not have the order receipt in front of them and could not tell the company what the number was. People spent a lot of extra time trying to locate an order before the problem-solving process could even begin. It's much easier to rearrange files according to the way requests are made; don't try to retrain your customers. The answer for this company was, obviously, to file according to customers' names.

Clearly type up headings such as "Advertising," "Agreements," "Bank," "Budget," "Contracts," "Duplicating Equipment," "Estimates," "Ideas," "Insurance"—all very basic and unmistakable.

Never, never, never tag a file "Miscellaneous"; it becomes a tempting dumping ground, and you won't remember where you've filed a "Misc.," nor will you remember what you filed in "Misc."

For pieces of paper that you really can't decide on immediately (are you sure?) set up a *rarely used* "Later" file. Beware: it's seductive! Be prepared next time you return to such a file to make decisions on what it contains: throw it away, file it, or act on it.

When training a subordinate or instructing co-workers in matters that continue to come up, keep a notebook and record the procedures as you go. It gives the person you're delegating to a permanent record and prevents numerous interruptions of your own time. You may also reuse it with additional or new employees.

## HOW TO SAVE TIME WITH TRAFFIC PATTERNS

File cabinets are most often placed near a secretary's desk. When I found that I used the files more than my secretary, I moved them into my own office, saving us both a lot of wasted time. *Be aware of who in your office does what,* and set up your office to ease the traffic flow, even if your particular arrangement looks crazy to outsiders. Their time is not at stake.

Arrange desks and working areas to minimize interruptions. Turn your desk so it doesn't face the open door. Have your secretary's back to the traffic to save her from unnecessary chit-chatters.

Set up your office so that the frequently used materials (calculators, paper, pens and pencils, specific books, whatever your job requires) are within reaching distance. You may want to put up one shelf on the wall nearest your desk, relegating infrequently used items to further recesses.

Common sense tells us to keep materials we use frequently in an accessible place, but when it comes to reference books and materials there is a tendency to alphabetize, which may lead to hunting for the most frequently needed materials on the top shelf or the most difficult-to-reach corner. A shelf designated only for often used material is the solution. Another may be to set a small cabinet or shelf near your desk for this material. It depends on how much material you have, the size of your office, and who else must use the material besides yourself.

## SETTING UP TIME-SAVING SYSTEMS AND PROCEDURES

We discussed that a strategy in the home is extremely important for accomplishing as much as possible; the same rule applies to the office. Often we perform a task in a certain way simply because it's always been done that way and worked. That doesn't necessarily make it the most effective method. Perhaps it's time to start rethinking ways certain jobs get done.

A company that hired me to work with them on the problem of taking orders over the telephone illustrates what can be wrong with "routine." This company had been using the same form and the same procedures for ten years. The procedure had always worked until the last year when business volume increased dramatically. I found an incredible amount of duplication of written material. It contaminated the whole place. Everybody kept reinventing the wheel: bookkeeping department, order fulfillment department, credit department, department files. The solution was simple. I helped the company devise a five-part form using NCR paper for the duplicates. Orders taken over the telephone were written once with all the information on one complete form and copies were distributed as needed.

This is a common problem many companies experience as business increases. Smart companies spot the problem immediately and take action.

## HOW TO SAVE TIME WITH CURRENT PRIORITIES

Depending on your job, you're going to have a certain number of deadlines, some daily, others monthly, etc. Keep track of impending deadlines with a comprehensive calendar of your choice. Often it is advisable to flag the deadline a few days before the due date.

Keep records of meetings, expenses, phone calls (where further action may be necessary), reports (dates assigned and dates due), and whatever else your particular business requires to offer quick reviews and year-end overall records. You may also want to keep this information in one daybook or a separate but easily accessible calendar.

Keep an updated Rolodex or card file. That's invaluable in networking. Even when you've only met someone once, if you've found it important enough to obtain name and number in the first place, then it's worth recording in one reference source, probably the Rolodex. If you can't remember names, file the person under her business: Quilts, Hospital Administration, Personnel Agency. *And do use the networking system.* Don't file and forget.

## HOW TO SAVE TIME COMMUTING

If you drive, consider investing in a cassette tape recorder. Remember: you can listen to best-sellers, learn French, take a business course, practice speeches, or singing—almost anything beats listening to radio commercials.

Many exercise books tell you how to make use of sitting time to firm up. Perhaps such tentative steps will lead you into more extensive programs.

Keep prestamped postcards or other notepaper in your purse or briefcase to jot down quick notes to friends and family. Of course you won't do this when driving, but when you're a passenger in a car, train, or plane, it's very convenient.

Catch up on your reading.

Decompress. Unwind from your business day and get set for your role as mother or wife (or vice versa). Commuting time is essential to many women to separate their roles and shift gears.

## HOW TO GET TIME FOR YOU—AT WORK

Many large corporations, aware of the necessity for their usually sedentary employees to get exercise, have set up gymnasiums or fitness programs—an excellent way to unwind during the course of the day and also to get in physical shape.

If you can't fit a cup of coffee and the newspaper into your morning schedule at home, try getting to work 15 minutes early and relaxing there. You're free of the at-home demands, and the office should be quiet enough for you to get set for the workday. You might also use this early office time to take care of work before normal hours and their bustle begin.

*Working Woman* magazine has published a list of "20 Ways to Spend Your Lunch Hour (Besides Eating)." A few of the best: Listen to music at free concerts (frequently provided in cities); see a short movie (often sponsored by museums and libraries);

join the YWCA and take advantage of its lunch-hour classes for working women—everyting from auto mechanics to dance; start a lunch-hour club—a great way to break into networking and spend time with friends; relax in a park—rent a horse or a bike, or just sit.

This lunch-hour break is an excellent time to unwind, enabling you to return to the office refreshed, rather than facing afternoon doldrums.

Most important: Recognize that there's always *time for you* if you know how to use it, not just the time left over at the end of the day.

# Husbands Are
# People, Too

Time with my husband is limited, but we recognize that and try to go by ourselves for three- and four-day week-ends about once a month; we review all the things that happen. We really try hard not to forget why we're doing all of these things in the first place.

—CHERYL HUGHES
*Independent consultant*

WHEN we don't control our time we tend to deal with it as one woman summed up beautifully: "Those things that scream the loudest are dealt with first."

The result: Time for us is the first to make way for the screamers; time for husbands is usually next. Husbands don't scream (usually): they're rational adults who understand that sometimes we just don't have time for them. Right?

To an extent, yes. But even the most understanding and rational husband is only going to be able to take so much neglect—no matter how benign—before he's going to start screaming for some attention, too.

It's a fact of life that women are working and their men are accepting it. So to prevent male screaming, don't cut too extensively into the time for him and give it to your children or work or friends. You probably guessed it: the key to making enough sensible (and fun) time for your husband is communication. You're right, he is a rational adult; but communication involves more than one-way messages telling him why you can't spend more time with him; it means discussing how you can spend more time together.

While you do need time to negotiate a mutually satisfactory solution, time together will be the payoff. So it's clearly an invaluable investment. It would be foolish to procrastinate; tomorrow he may be gone with the wind and your success at work won't taste so good.

Cheryl Hughes made an important point when she said she and her husband did not want to lose sight of what they were doing everything *for*—working at demanding jobs, balancing home and office, and so forth. They're doing it all because they want a *quality of life* that will enable them to enjoy each other, their daughter, and their home. And if they don't take their weekends together to review events they could very easily lose sight of that priority value.

Until women started working, men were financially responsible for the entire family. Women may complain about how much housework they did and how difficult it was to raise the children alone when their husbands were at work all day (and it *is* a demanding job), but the responsibility of supporting the family was hardly easy.

## THE MALE BURDENS ARE EASING

With the early battles over, men are realizing that with the burden eased by their two-paycheck marriages, they can relax a bit. Some can even afford to quit a job they hate; they don't *have* to strive for the top job which may mean they're now working shorter hours; they come home to wives who are interesting and interested in things other than home and children.

And they like it. So, despite all the initial statistics that showed nonsupportive husbands refusing to help with housework, jealous of their wives' jobs, and threatened by their wives' earning capacity, we're now seeing more and more husbands supportive because they like having pressures lifted and are willing to help a wife ease her own multirole pressures.

You shouldn't be afraid to talk to your husband about these pressures. Smart women are realizing that, having won equality with men, they should cooperate with their particular men as equals. They are investing the time it takes to communicate and working out equitable situations—each as different as the couples involved—that work for them, easing the time pressures on both.

## A COUNSELOR'S VIEW

Dr. Sarah Slagle, herself a working mother and wife, counsels working couples and has observed changing attitudes:

"There's no question that women moving into the work force have changed the traditional family structure enormously. I don't think we realize as a society the extent to which this change has already taken place. If you ask how people are reacting to these changes I see much variability, depending, I think, on where they were in their life cycle when these changes began to take place. The younger couples I see in New York City are working out more egalitarian relationships from the beginning of their marriages with respect to sharing household tasks and children. Most of these men I've come in contact with are glad that their wives wish to pursue careers. It makes them more interesting people, and it shifts some of the financial responsibility off the man.

"The couples I see in the suburbs who were older when these

changes began to occur often do have more conflict as a couple. It's harder to change an established pattern. A man who's been used to his wife being home and taking care of everything on the domestic front for many years is more apt to feel threatened when this changes.

"A friend of ours whose wife began working after being home with their children for several years experienced a great deal of loneliness when his wife was away. (His work permitted him to be home at odd times during the day.) He confided to us once that he used to go down to the station and look at her car, he felt so badly! He could wax poetic, exclaiming: 'When Anna is in the kitchen cooking, I know our ship is going forward.'

"That was a couple of years ago. More recently he's talked to my husband and myself about the enormous relief he's experienced at not being the sole supporter of his family. Now if something happened to him, the ship could go forward much more readily than before."

Dr. Slagle has also observed that communication often turns up the fact that men don't want their wives to be Superwomen—and that women don't necessarily want their husbands to be Supermen.

"I think to get away from the need to be Superwomen," she says, "we have to help men get away from the need society has so frequently placed on them to be Supermen. My own thinking on this is that if a husband and wife set out to develop a workable division of labor so the wife doesn't have to be Superwoman with the accompanying fatigue and discontent, they can do it. It may mean that the husband is encouraged by the wife not to take the top-level management job that requires him to travel one week out of four and work ten-hour days. A couple who set out to develop this kind of balance in their family life and work life will find a lot of interest and challenge in it, and find their own relationship growing.

"I'm in this situation myself and what it takes is sitting down—

rather frequently—and doing a lot of talking about what's working well and what still needs to be modified. A sample mini-discussion in our house recently went something like this: 'I'm not too happy with the way the boys are looking going off to school in the morning.' 'Well, if we just got up 15 minutes earlier, you'd have time to lay out clothes for them while I'm getting breakfast, and there won't be that mad dash getting out of the house.' That was a breakfast-cooking father's suggestion, and so far it's working quite well.

"This is an example of a detail. Forging a basic structure took hours and hours of discussing aims, priorities, and what's important to each of us. It also takes frequent evaluations of how the boys are doing, how we're doing, planning vacations that fit the needs of both of us. Having to map out a new pattern forces one to think about priorities in a way that the traditional marriages never did."

## TWO-WAY PRIORITIES

Communication, always a two-way street, is not always easy, but obviously pays off. If you're living with someone, include that person in your own priority-setting sessions. Obviously, if your family is your first thought in your quality of life plan, it would be self-defeating not to include your mate in that planning session. Superwoman again?

With sources as different as *Cosmopolitan* magazine and Betty Friedan urging women to recognize husbands as equal partners and the importance of creating unpressured time together, it's a difficult message to resist:

*Plan time with your husband.*

It may seem silly to make "dates" with the man you've already married, but taking a partner for granted gradually pushes man and woman farther apart until it's too late.

The women who do schedule time for their husbands either have saved faltering marriages or are still romantically in love with their men.

In addition to their regular weekends together, for example, Cheryl Hughes's "favorite treat" is to "arrange it so sometimes I stay down in the city and meet my husband after work and go out to dinner or play tennis."

Free-lance illustrator Genevieve Meek and her husband *always* have dinner with each other, no matter how late they work.

Margo Berk-Levine, who owns two personnel agencies, observed: "We discovered after the second child that we began to lose touch. I realized that we absolutely had to take one night a week even if it was to just take a walk or whatever to just spend the time away from the children that was for *us*. You tend to get so involved with everything else that you suddenly realize it's been a month since you've really talked to each other. We instituted one specific night a week, because I found if we didn't, there was always something else that came up. Now there's Margo and Al time."

Berk-Levine relates a story that reflects the changes in attitude:

"Al was not too happy about the live-in help at first. All these changes, and suddenly there was also somebody else cooking. There were nights Al would come home and the housekeeper was there and dinner was ready, but I might not be there. They were growth changes for both of us. I was feeling more professional, more successful, more interested in being with the business; I also felt it was important to get involved with the children's school. We went through a period after one of our sleep-in housekeepers left of trying to have somebody come in and leave after she did the dinner dishes. One night she left while we were still eating dinner and that night I was putting the dishes into the dishwasher and getting the pots ready and I hadn't really given it a thought, and suddenly Al turned to me and said, 'What are you doing? Why should *you*, after a full day's work, be doing the dishes and the pots?' I thought, "*My, how we have changed!*"

The change came so slowly that Berk-Levine's husband wasn't even aware of it until she pointed it out to him later. And he admitted he had indeed changed; his priorities were more in sync with his wife's.

## WHAT TO DO WITH HIM

In addition to communication, here are some specific things you can do to make time with your husband:

*Plan a night*, a weekend, a week together *alone*—get in touch, review your lives—separate and together. Renew priorities, enjoy each other. This together time can be as simple as an evening at a restaurant (pay a baby-sitter to stay with the children) or a cruise for two to a romantic island.

*Allow spontaneity* to play a part in your relationship with your husband just as you would anything else. Forget the dishes and take a walk together. Is it rational to be so inflexible about housekeeping that you sacrifice time with your husband?

*Pick priorities:* What's the best use of my time right now? Doing the laundry or talking with my husband?

*Pay a housekeeper* so you'll have more time for your husband. If you can't afford help, combine your chores with time for him. Remember Cheryl Hughes and her after-dinner family hour. But work with your husband on this: ask for his help, don't demand it; take into consideration the responsibilities he's already handling that you're not concerned with (car maintenance, yard upkeep, heavy-duty house repairs); don't demand perfectionism of him, just as you're learning not to demand it of yourself.

*Send the children to a friend's,* relative's, or co-op member's house for the evening (repay in kind or with another service) and have the evening alone with him, free of conflicts.

The time you spend with your husband should be a relaxing, enjoyable part of your life. It does neither of you any good if that time is spent with one eye on the clock. With both eyes on each other, you won't lose sight of what you're doing it all for.

# Making Time for Sex

---

> You can get a lot of satisfaction out of a job, but it's awfully nice to have a warm body next to you once in a while.
>
> —VICKI RIKER
> *Media director*

WE DON'T MEAN to imply by our separation of the chapters on husbands and sex that the two are mutually exclusive. Hopefully not! But time for sex is just as important for us women without husbands as it is for those with, so . . .

Time for sex is a two-part dilemma:

First, if you're as busy as the rest of us, where do you find the time to meet the man?

And second, once you meet someone, when do you find the time to develop and pursue your relationship?

(By sex, incidentally, I'm not just talking about the act of sexual intercourse, but also the intimacy and ability to simply *be with* someone of the opposite sex.)

The most common response to both questions was:

"I *make* time."

As with anything else, women check out their priorities and if dating, sex, relationships—whatever you want to call it—is important to them, they find time in their schedules.

"Because romance is a high priority," says Liz Wolff, a teacher, "I do schedule it in. My special male friend and I definitely have one night a week to go out by ourselves or do something by our-selves, whether it's in my environment or his. We try to have some special time where we can go to the beach or something like that by ourselves."

To be honest, when we began interviewing women for this book, we expected that single women would have more conflicts than married women, if only because they didn't have the emotional support of a husband. Surprisingly, except for admitting to the loneliness that sometimes sneaks up on them when there's nobody around to talk to, most single women said they had *fewer* conflicts. Both divorced and never married women said the lack of a permanent relationship lessens strains on them because there was one less person placing continuing demands on their time, as a husband does (whether he intends to or not).

"In a dating relationship," continued Wolff, "when you're to-gether you're *really* together; you schedule it and you look forward to it. It's sort of uncluttered."

Many of the men we date have also been through marriages and divorces, and value their own time as much as we value ours. They make fewer demands on the women they date because there is more of an effort going on to be considerate of each other's con-flicts: the children, the job, the household demands—on his front as well as yours.

Meeting men is much simpler for some women than for others. As you'd expect, there is a direct correlation in the jobs the women held with the number (and quality) of men they meet. It figures: women who work in male-dominated corporations or businesses tend to meet more men because their work arena puts them in daily contact with males.

What about women in traditionally female occupations with fewer male co-workers? Rosalie Davies, a school librarian, is in this situation, yet she places a high priority on dating:

"I have to make time to go out to meet people. I find that a good little Protestant midwestern girl like myself, raised in a very strait-laced home, is now in a completely different world. I do go to singles bars. In fact, that's where I've met some of my most interesting mates. I've also met some very dull people there. Ninety percent of my time is wasted, but when I'm really lonely, then I have to go somewhere; I almost have to force myself."

## USING SINGLES BARS

Forget *Looking for Mr. Goodbar*. Singles bars are as safe as you are mature. If you act silly and vulnerable, you could get in trouble. But if you're responsible and perceptive, there's no reason you should be either nervous or ashamed about occasionally visiting a singles bar to meet men. That's what they're for. I probably never would have thought to list singles bars as a time-saver, but that's exactly what they are: effective ways to meet men in a busy life where other avenues prove impossible.

Just because you visit such a bar doesn't mean you're there for instant sex, a one-night stand, or whatever. And as long as you make your own objectives clear, such public meeting places are indicative of the changing times and new needs.

## THE CASE FOR CASUAL SEX

One woman who ranks sex high, if not first, on her list of priorities, believes: "I've planned that much better than I've planned my business. When I went into business, I said I can't have a relationship and a business at the same time. There's not enough time to combine both successfully. So mostly, I hate to say this, it's casual sex and no relationships at all. I haven't made a *date* in about seven years, because most of the people I go out with are friends who I have sex with simply because I don't have the time to develop a relationship on another level.

"I go out disco dancing because I can get very lonely. I think I have a very male attitude toward almost everything. I can pick up a guy and take him home and never see him again. I trained myself to do that because I'm not a woman who functions well without a man. A friend gave me the idea to 'build a stable.' I first thought she was crazy. But what happens if you really do have a stable of about five guys—you don't love them all and some are more special—you get some sort of consistency because every five weeks one of them will call you. They're not good for consistency in and of themselves, but if you get enough, then you have a steady social life. It takes a long time."

## WHY IT WORKS

This may seem rather calculated. We're not making moral judgments nor are we condemning or condoning her way of life. But it's a textbook example of time management:

She thought about her quality-of-life values and decided social life was important.

She set her goals, which included a steady, sexually satisfied life to be fulfilled by a five-man stable.

She planned activities to achieve these goals, such as going disco dancing (where she did, in fact, meet one of her five).

She continually checks out her priorities and, having achieved her satisfactory social life system, she is now free to concentrate on her business.

## BEING MORE SELECTIVE

Our busy schedules also teach us to be more selective with our choice of men and the time we schedule to see them. The result is frequently "quality" relationships equivalent to the "quality" time we give our children. We're no longer as interested in adding notches to our belt as we are in making our time with men count.

Ava Stern, publisher of *Enterprising Women,* values supportive men with a sense of humor: "Those are the kind of people I prefer to be with once a week or even once a month rather than somebody I feel guilty about not being with more often. I know this is a lonelier route, but it's a better one for me. Those times are very special—I'm never too tired for sex when it's with someone who has a sense of humor and can play along with whatever's going on."

Stern further points out the value of quality time: "I think the people I know who have weekend marriages are very good at it because they tend to concentrate their work during the week and their play during the weekend. I think that could be a lot of fun. I could do that."

Some women, though they value male relationships, still feel torn by their other responsibilities. "I'm starting to go out more now," says Gail Buchalter, the free-lance writer, "and I feel worse about it. I'm leaving my son, and I'm wondering how much time I should be giving him. I give him a lot of concentrated time from when I pick him up at school till I go out. I also make sure to stay home a few nights a week, and we play and have discussions. I love my nights at home—they're totally to myself. When Jordan's asleep, I read or watch TV or listen to records."

When Buchalter does go out, however, her perspective changes: "At that point, I've obviously made my decision; there's no point in not having a good time. And I usually do. If it's an enjoyable situation, I don't worry. I don't call home every 20 minutes like I used to. I leave numbers where I can be reached, and that's it."

Women who make this time for dating and being with friends all do it for the same reason: fun and relaxation. They consider it important time for themselves without which they would feel frustrated and one-dimensional.

Says Rosalie Davies: "I find that if I don't let go or if I don't have time to be foolish or time to create things I need to create— if I don't make that time, I feel that life is not worth living. I get that way very easily, so those times are very important to me."

Davies, who told us she does get tired frequently, also said that dating seems to renew her energy. Going out to dinner or to the theater can be relaxing after a hard day at work.

## HOW WORKING STIMULATES SEX

Summoning the energy for a physical act such as sex can be something else altogether. Dr. Doris Moss has observed another side to this:

"The woman always was tired; she always had the proverbial headache. Now she may be less tired. A lot of that headache and a lot of the tiredness from years back were from those ladies who were frustrated and bored and resentful. They were stuck at home with nothing to stimulate them even to thinking about sex, about having physical relationships. Now we have the lady who's had a hell of a good day in her career, her adrenaline's flowing, something really great has happened that day, she's excited about a deal she's consummated or something's on the fire. She's been speaking to men and women all day in situations that she finds stimulating and challenging. She may come home ready to have that nice cocktail and relax and she still has energy to work off. So that's looking at it in a *positive* way. That kind of energy can really give you the impetus to have sexual relationships—something good.

"What about the other lady? Those days where nothing is terrible, but nothing is great either? You've put in a long day and you're tired. It comes back to communication. If your sexual relationship with your mate is a good one, there has to be some communication anyway and hopefully you're not having sex just because it's every other Thursday night; hopefully you're tuned in to each other's little clues. How do people communicate with each other, for sharing needs and moods and feelings and emotions?

"One of the things, of course, is feedback and response. If we don't share our feelings, how can our mates know what we're even thinking or feeling? How can they second-guess us? Unless they have X-ray vision. So then, you can't complain that your spouse isn't being responsive to your mood, like 'Can't you see that I really don't feel like it?' if you haven't shared that you really don't feel like it. It's not a rejection of him, number one, and it could just be time when 'I'd like to have you to touch and comfort, to just kind of relax.'

"In a new relationship, where you're first setting the patterns for communication, it's even more important to be as open as you can. You're not going to reveal all your sexual needs, desires and feelings to someone on the first night you've met him. But presumably, if it's going to be a relationship of any importance, you reach a point where you start to be open and communicative with each other, hopefully the earlier on the better. The problem with most people is they start off that way, then at some point it dries up or turns off and we can't communicate with each other. Of course, there's communication and communication. Sometimes I think communication is overworked, too, where everything is so analyzed, every emotion, every feeling, every response—'What did you mean by that? Did you mean what I think you meant?' Coming back to the word 'spontaneity'—enjoy each other without hashing and rehashing."

## THE SEX SCHEDULE

Once again we see how setting priorities and good communication play an invaluable role in finding time—including time for sex. Here are a few specific steps to find additional time:

Schedule time to be alone with your partner. Scheduling isn't making appointments for sexual liaisons. It reminds you that there should be a time for sex; it frees up some time; as with any schedule, there should be flexibility, and this flexibility should help you to relax.

Planning a date with someone special ahead of time gives you something to look forward to during the day. You know you're not going to work late because of the date, which can be an entire evening of time for you. Starting with a luxurious bath (interruption-free) helps to build a romantic atmosphere.

The planning (anticipating crises, setting priorities and so forth) also helps to put confidence into your life, confidence that if your mate comes home and is feeling romantic, you can have the spontaneous response of saying "This is more important to me than washing clothes tonight." Or an early morning response might be "It's OK now; we just won't have a big breakfast and everything else is running smoothly; what's more fun, anyway?"

If you're in control of your life there will always be time for romance. Scheduling sex for every other Thursday is hardly romantic, but making dates with your husband or special friend is.

Such dates may be a quiet rendezvous at a romantic restaurant, a weekend for two on a friend's houseboat, or a spontaneous walk after dinner. What's important is that you make the time to maintain the intimacy you've developed with your mate and that you keep (or put) romance into your life.

Examine current habits. Are too many cocktails and too much TV putting you out of the mood and wasting time you might rather spend having a relationship with someone?

Be aware of your peak periods. Many of the women who amazed us with their energy simply schedule their social life for late at night when they've unwound from work, taken care of business at home, and been hit by a new surge of energy. Many of us have such energy peaks that could be much better used to date than to dust and dust.

Time for sex is not frivolous. Nor is it sleazy. It's definitely part of time for you.

# The Children's Hour

It didn't work out like we thought—that it would be just like before plus a baby. That was a very naive assumption.

—CINDY ANNCHILD
*Co-owner, the Bath House*

PROBLEMS with controlling your time increase substantially—need we say it?—when there are children. And since each mother's relationship with (and values for) her own children is intensely individual, it's a difficult problem to address with generalizations. The basic time problems regarding children are obvious:

*Time to have children:* Is there a *right* time to have children? Before we start our careers? Time out once our careers have been established? When is it *safe* to make children our main priority?

*Time without the children:* Child-care arrangements are consistently cited as the major problem of working mothers. Unless you're satisfied that your child is receiving good care when away from you, you're not going to be 100 percent effective.

*Time with the children:* Quality time versus quantity time is a major issue. Many mothers are realizing the value of quality time; others find the balance difficult. What, they ask, does quality time really mean?

Now that women can relax their single-minded push to work,

they realize other things exist that they consider important, such as having children. With a definite biological time limit on having children, many women feel they've either missed their chance or had better hurry up. The emphasis on the working woman role has shifted; the new emphasis is on the family.

Betty Friedan wrote in the *New York Times:* "What is beginning to concern me even more today is the conflicts women now suffer as they reach 30 or 35 and cannot choose to have a child. I don't envy younger women who are facing or denying that agonizing choice we won for them. Because it isn't really a free choice when their paycheck is needed to cover the family bills each month, when women must look to their jobs and professions for the security and status their mothers once sought in marriage alone, and when these professions are not structured for people who give birth to children and take responsibility for their upbringing.

"Most of us let ourselves be seduced into giving up our careers in order to embrace motherhood, and it wasn't easy to resume them. We told our daughters that they could—and should— have it all. Why not? After all, men do. But the *Superwomen* who are trying to *have it all*, combining full-time careers and *stretch-time* motherhood, are enduring such relentless pressure that their younger sisters may not even dare to think about having children."

All is not grim, however. Society is taking notice of the drop in the birthrate. The desire to have children (and the problems inherent in having them in a working society) is encouraging changes to alleviate the time problems of pregnancy (time off work) and raising children.

Most solutions must come from the business world, since it's been the most inflexible about time, thereby creating the problems. We can always juggle husband, children, home, and selves to *some* extent, but if a boss or a company policy says "Nine to five or else," the juggling act becomes lopsided.

Fortunately, some businesses have recognized the problem and are attempting to work out solutions that will enable working mothers to balance their home and office lives. From corporations to individual employers, the solutions are innovative and effective. Results are so positive in most cases that many observers feel it's only a matter of time—how much time?—before most of business is geared toward a balanced family-work situation.

## THE NEW PART-TIMER

Part-time work is beginning to mean more than working 20 hours a week at a fast-food eatery, then trying to make do on the so-called "salary." It now includes women who have approached employers to work out restricted hours at the office with flexibility (not always leaving promptly at noon), plus perhaps some work at home, where they can be with their children.

It includes a mother and father taking turns working and caring for the children: the mother may work at a job in the morning, the father in the afternoon, and each one's child-care time coincides with the other's working time.

It includes more formal experiments, such as one in five New York school systems permitting two teachers to share one elementary-school class, letting them split the full salary, with one teacher working in the morning and the other in the afternoon. The experiment has been a huge success and will be expanded.

Most such experiments in part-time careers have produced positive results for employers (productivity and enthusiasm are high with shorter hours, turnover is low) as well as employees (conflicts between home and office are minimized, relieving stress and permitting a healthier family life, while still yielding money and personal fulfillment). This system of part-time work has not caught on nationally yet, but legislation has been introduced around the country to pave the way to more and more of this solution.

Meanwhile, if the idea appeals to you, check out your personal situation: Would it be possible in your job? Are you willing to give up the complete immersion in your eight-hour days? Would the part-time solution be right for your child-care problems? Can you approach your employer about the possibility?

If you think this may work for you, lay out all pluses and minuses *before* going to your employer; consider his own problems (employee benefits and so forth).

## WHO'S GOT FLEXTIME?

What about flextime? With flexibility always the key to effective time management, it would seem inevitable that corporations would begin to institute the system: employees work at the office or factory during a midday core of hours, arranging their arrival, departure, and lunchtimes according to personal needs. The system is not new; its effectiveness in European countries has been studied for many years. Profitability and productivity are up, absenteeism down.

So why isn't everybody doing it? There's always been a strong resistance to change of any sort, and the traditional 40-hour work week is so entrenched as "the only way" that many businesses simply refuse to consider options. It's often up to individuals, such as yourself, to present the idea.

If you can convince the boss to let you try it, prove to him that it's just as effective as all the reports claim.

Again, the change is gradual, but it's there. The National Council for Alternative Work Patterns has even compiled a directory of 290 businesses that offer flextime, part-time, and job sharing. The directory is available in libraries and colleges; it sells for $25 (1925 K St., N.W., Suite 308A, Washington, D.C. 20006).

Flexible working programs should ease the decision to have children. Knowing that you can be home at certain times and that your balancing act won't be too precarious should make the time to have children *your* choice again.

But what about *now* if you already have children and there's no way you can work out a tenable part-time situation?

A Working Mothers Research Project, funded by the Department of Health, Education, and Welfare and conducted by Dr. Sheila Kamerman, senior research associate at Columbia University, labeled child care as "overwhelmingly the most serious problem experienced by such women. The paucity of adequate child-care services at reasonable cost leads parents to make multiple and complicated arrangements to assure good care while they are at work."

## PARENTING SUBSTITUTES

It doesn't take a study for most of us to be aware of the problems with child care. The pursuit of good arrangements *and* the subsequent concern about the quality of the care are very, very serious time-wasters.

Finding satisfactory child care for your children (and your own peace of mind) is a matter of thoroughly investigating what's available. Unless you feel you have done adequate research and chosen the *best*, you won't perform well in your job and personal relationships.

Happily, the problem is receiving growing attention and

options are increasing and improving. If you have no idea where to begin looking for child-care arrangements, rely on your *network*. Reading can prove to be a time-saver as more books and magazine articles tackle the child-care problem. A book we found particularly helpful (in this and other subjects) is *The Working Mother's Complete Handbook* by Gloria Norris and JoAnn Miller (E. P. Dutton/Sunrise).

Child-care arrangements can be formal or informal. The formal include traditional day-care systems: government-funded, profit-making, private nonprofit, and nursery school. All have disadvantages and advantages and we're not even going to attempt to tell you what to look for since we honestly believe that one woman's curse would be another woman's blessing. At any rate, you'll be sure to examine each situation carefully, keeping your own priorities clear in your mind.

Less formal child-care arrangements are largely a result of increasing demands for more flexible, personalized child care and can often be adapted to suit you and your child. They include:

*Sitter:* Many working women have found women with children of their own who want to work but do not want to leave their own children; they have solved this problem by taking care of friends' children for a fee. Although such situations may eventually develop into day-care centers for these women, it usually remains a personalized care system. Sitters also include full-time housekeepers who care for a child in your home and part-time help after school hours or when the children are sick and you must go to work.

*Husband:* If you haven't already worked out coparenting, you can probably count on your husband for emergency child care. More men are taking an active interest in their children's welfare (changing societal values) and are willing to stay home with children when possible.

*Relatives:* We don't think your mother and mother-in-law is the ideal primary child-care system (sometimes this creates friction and you must remember your mother already raised her children and may want to get on with her own life). But relatives can sometimes help out in a pinch and sometimes prove the best system for your child. Think of the ramifications before enlisting such close-to-home help.

*Baby-sitting co-ops:* These often apply only to after-work hours but they prove invaluable. They often involve an exchange of time, so you must be sure you're willing to trade time for time. Co-ops can also be valuable if you have fairly flexible hours or you work at home and know other women who also work at home.

*The office baby:* Again, consider your personal situation and the possibility of bringing your child to work. Women business owners feel freer to use this child-care than others, but the idea is creeping into office situations as well. Much of the success depends on the age and personality of the baby. Quiet infants are obviously going to work out better than noisy, inquisitive two-year-olds. Both Judy Sommerschield and Cindy Annchild bring their children to their own businesses; it occasionally causes problems, but the overall benefits have been worth it. For the most part, the two women and others like them have found that even customers respond well to "a child in the business."

Despite the overall "rigidity and unresponsiveness of the workplace" noted in the Kamerman study, some businesses have shown an interest and begun innovations in child care that, we hope, will lead other workplaces to do the same. Corporate child care has proved successful at the Stride Rite Corporation in Boston, where both employees and neighborhood parents can use on-premise facilities. The Amalgamated Clothing and Textile Workers Union has been including provisions in its contracts for child-care nurseries on factory premises. One of the earliest such experiments, at a textile factory in the South, showed that the women workers' productivity increased when their children were nearby.

"Corporate child care" is my personal favorite because it's one-stop, an invaluable time-saver. It also lets you have car time and lunch with your children, important opportunities to talk heart to heart.

Other corporations are following suit; again, it's a slow change, but it's happening and it'll continue if women make their needs known. It may involve an investment of your time, and to be truthful, you may never see the results in time for your own children, but the "younger sisters" mentioned in Betty Friedan's article may be direct beneficiaries of our efforts.

Large corporations are not the only businesses doing something about child care for their employees. In downtown St. Louis 15 smaller businesses have combined resources with child-care professionals and working parents to create a nonprofit child-care center for preschool children. Results: lower absenteeism, higher productivity, lower turnover among the employees using the center.

Networking can help you find *and* help you create such alternative solutions to child care. We're not optimistically dismissing child care, which is a very real problem for working mothers; all is not yet roses. But the options are so varied and responsiveness to the need has become so much more widespread in just a few years that we feel optimum child-care services are no longer an elusive goal.

## QUALITY VERSUS QUANTITY TIME

If you're not happy with your arrangements you're going to feel guilty about leaving your child, no matter how much working means to you. If you're happy with the outside care your child is receiving, there's no reason to feel guilty. Remember, doing your best is as close as we're expected to come to being Super-women.

Not only will we be more effective at work, with one thing less to worry about, but also the time we do spend with our children will vastly improve. No longer will you need to feel that you must prove you're still his mother, you still love him, etc. You can concentrate on having a good time and imparting the values you want your children to learn.

What about quality time versus quantity time with children? Many women say they understand the premise—that the *way* you spend the little time you have with your children can be much more important than the number of hours; but they still find it difficult to accept that together time is so limited.

"The business of quality time being more important than quantity time," says Rosemary Gaillard, a very quality-oriented mother of two girls who works at a family service agency, "stands up to a degree, but sometimes you can't have the quality you want without the quantity. There are times when I wish it was me who could sit down in the middle of the morning and read stories; many times I wish I could have her with me or be hanging around her while I'm doing the household responsibilities or daytime things. There are times when her nursery school goes on field trips, and I'd like to be one of the mothers who can accompany them and watch them learning."

Instead, the mothers need to make the most of the time they do have with their children, which isn't always easy. Many of the women are angry about the unresponsiveness of school systems to the increasing number of working mothers. Liz Wolff, herself a teacher, expresses this:

"I've explained to my children that I don't have time to come when they have a little talent program at two in the afternoon. You always have the feeling of guilt, but that usually subsides. And you do have a choice—you could take the afternoon off. It depends on your priorities at the time. The second feeling is anger, the assumption being that you're sitting home all day long doing nothing but popping bonbons. Today there are a lot of working mothers and I don't know where the school system is coming from!"

## YOU CAN KEEP IN TOUCH

Wolff advises working mothers to make contact with their children's teachers; write notes—and expect replies—when something happens with your children that you feel the teacher should be aware of (going out of town, home problems or events, anything that may affect the child's work or behavior); let the principal know where to reach you; ask the teacher to keep you informed of your child's progress with specifics (such as: needs help in math, improved greatly in English).

Another time-saving tip: Ask for a complete schedule of the year's school activities in September—the Christmas play, PTA meetings, Easter egg hunt, and other activities are usually set in advance. This will help you immensely in planning your own schedule.

Working mothers almost unanimously agree on the importance of teaching children the value of communication. If the child is aware of a school function, he is taught to tell his mother immediately, not on the day of the event. Continued disappointment when a child's short notice makes it impossible for his mother to attend eventually teaches the importance of such information.

Notes Dr. Sarah Slagle: "An unsolved problem for many women is still the conflict between career and children. I think most women will have a hard time choosing between these two options—most will still choose to do both. Indeed, for many women with children, our inflated economy gives them no choice but to work. For mothers with school-age children and reasonable support from their mates and the community, this problem is much less. In fact impressive research on the effects of maternal employment reviewed by Lois Hoffman in a recent issue of *The American Psychologist* indicated that school-age children of women who're employed fared better than children of nonworking mothers on many dimensions such as increased independence."

We've noticed that mothers who recognize that positive personality traits have developed in their children since they began working are the mothers who have their own priorities straight; do not confuse their children with guilt; and give their children additional responsibility which makes the children feel they're a vital part of their mother's success and happiness—which, of course, they are.

"I see what most women do not allow themselves," sighs Rosemary Gaillard, "and their children are screwed up and they want to know why. If you don't take care of yourself, you're teaching your children that you're not worth anything, so that's the example; they grow up thinking they're not worth enough to give attention to themselves! I think the role model is very important."

## HOW TO MAKE MORE TIME WITH YOUR CHILDREN

Here are specific steps you can take to increase the time you have with your children and the quality of time:

Delegate responsibilities to your children that they can handle and that make them feel good. Often housecleaning can become a family affair, itself quality time; the help will make it go more quickly and increase playtime.

Make lunch dates with your children much as you would with husband or friends. Gaillard goes home for lunch almost every day; it's exhausting but worth it, she feels. She also found that her husband (she's separated) will share lunchtime with the children, freeing her to enjoy lunch with friends occasionally. Another woman arranged for her children to attend school near her office so they can be together on the way to work, have lunch together, and plan after-work, after-school hours on the way home.

Use your morning time to be with your children. If everything is well planned and you can get up 15 minutes earlier, this can be a peaceful time to talk and enjoy each other while dressing and eating breakfast, rather than a hectic time when you barely have a moment to say "Good morning."

Use chauffeur time to enjoy your children. Sure, sometimes it's annoying to be constantly shuttling youngsters back and forth, but if you look at it positively, as a time for one-on-one relationships with individual children or a time to get to know your child's playmates better, you can upgrade the chore to "quality" time.

Take the phone off the hook. If you want Saturday mornings or dinner hours free of interruptions, this trick ensures it. Women who have tried it find that it vastly increases the quality of time they have with their children; those who don't do it wish they did.

Share your children with your husband; after all, he played a part in their being around. Plan dinners or outings together. Let daddy take them to the library on Saturday morning while you sleep late (or you use this time to plan your week). If you don't like movies and your husband does, let him take the children to an occasional film.

When you travel, pay a little bit more attention to the children just before and right after the trip. Postcards from far-off places where mom is (with an X marking the spot) are always appreciated. Discuss with your children where you're going and why. Perhaps a gift on the return home would be nice (though some people view gifts as bribes or conscience soothers, traveling fathers have come back bearing gifts for centuries with no noticeable damage).

Let your children know you're always available, whether at work or on a trip. This makes your not being there a lot less frightening; most children, if you train them right, will not abuse the privilege of using the phone to call you.

If possible, bring your children to work at least once, so they'll have a good idea of what you're doing and where. It helps children appreciate your "other role."

One great idea, from *Cosmopolitan,* is to give your children an inexpensive camera and have them take snapshots of themselves, friends, and the family to show you when you've been away. This should be just as much fun for you as for them, since you'll be able to see a little of what you've "missed."

Elevator company owner/operator Marie McDonald, whose own children are now adults, still wonders what the *right* way is to combine children and career:

"I've thought, looking back, that because I didn't give my children the attention they needed or that I now wish I had, I look at my daughters and think, *What should you do? How are you going to have both the career, if you want one, and the children?* My oldest daughter has one son, and she's planning to be a chiropractor. With one child, she's pretty well planned her time so she could spend a good deal of time with him. At one point, she even worked only part-time, to be home when he came home from school. She worked all the time he was little and always had sitters. That's the route she went.

"I've given a lot of thought to what would be the ideal. And I may be wrong, but I think when we have children, if being a mother and homemaker were given the value it should be given, more of us might be willing to invest those first 10 to 15 years to having children and not try to juggle it so much; and *then* we'd go back. There are a lot of men who in World War II spent five or more years in the service and then went to college; it didn't seem to hurt their career at all. It's more a matter, I think, of dedication and feeling serious about what we're doing. Women aren't valued as homemakers or mothers, yet philosophically I can't think of a more important function for a person than to raise another human being."

# Time Off for Vacations

When it's vacation time, don't talk to me—I'm leaving. I
think vacations are an essential part of being successful.
— SUSAN SCHEIN
*Owner, public relations firm*

VACATION TIME: for children, it's visions of Mickey Mouse
and Disneyworld, swimming and skinned knees; for adults, it's
visions of an island in the Caribbean, a mountain in Colorado . . .

For too many of us, vacations remain visions. We either put
off or don't take vacations because we tell ourselves, "Look how
much I can get done if I don't go!"

Bluntly, that's insanity. An auto workers' study for contract
renewal turned up that a minimum of three weeks' vacation is required to restore workers' souls: Unwind the first week; get used
to being on vacation the second; enjoy yourself the third.

Although not many companies provide three-week relief, it's
essential to your good health to make use of what time you can
take. I know one woman who has put off her vacation for two
years because her boss keeps telling her, "We can't make it without you." She believes it. Her male co-workers, however, have
never missed a vacation, and somehow the office has muddled
through without them (she is, by the way, the only woman in
the office). She is also, at this point, an unhappy nervous wreck.

All too often we tend to believe in our indispensability. Just as we must recognize that our home life will not fall apart when we're working, we must learn that the office will not fall apart if we take time off.

The women who most enjoy their vacations are those who apply the principles of time management to their office situations while they're working. They have delegated their responsibilities, trained their subordinates, and kept the office in good enough order to be able to leave knowing that things will carry on fairly normally.

Hotel sales manager Donna Davis, for example, plays just as hard as she works. Because her time is not her own at work, she works long hours. She does not take three-week vacations, but has worked out an enviable "time-off" schedule and is, she says, "famous for my three-day weekends":

"The reason I take the time off is because it's good for me to get away from the hotel and from the business, and see what other people are doing and just relax and play tennis and soak up some sunshine. . . . I'm an outdoors person. Our hours are such that it's seven or eight in the morning until midnight many days a week. Often we work Saturdays and Sundays. Our management people realize we've got to have time off at some point. And I'd rather take a Friday or a Monday and make a long weekend out of it than take an entire week or two weeks, unless I were to go to Europe or some place where you need the time to go.

"I'm mentally capable of leaving and not calling the hotel, not checking on anything as long as I've taken care of everything before I leave, and forgetting about the business for a little while and just reading or writing poetry or jogging up and down the beach or playing tennis—whatever is available for wherever I am."

## WHAT TO DO BEFOREHAND

The key to enjoying your vacation is being sure everything in the office has been taken care of. Vacations are no fun when you're calling in constantly or available to co-workers for questions.

(The tips in the section on traveling for business also apply to vacations.)

If you work for a company, your vacation time should be specified before you take the job: one week or two weeks or whatever. To ensure yourself an enjoyable vacation, you should plan it far enough in advance to enable you to:

Avoid conflicts with co-workers' plans

Make any travel arrangements in advance (especially if your trip will fall during the holidays when airlines are overbooked months ahead of time. Airlines also provide substantial discounts for preplanners)

Get your work done or into good enough shape that you'll feel comfortable leaving the office for two weeks

Handle problems that arise, perhaps even juggling your vacation time, but *never* canceling it

Marie McDonald, for example, always checks the schedule for the conventions of two elevator associations she belongs to. Then she and her husband make plans to attend the conventions and combine them with vacation time.

Planning in advance enables you to synchronize your plans with those of a friend or husband with whom you might want to travel.

Business owners and free-lancers seem to have more trouble planning vacation time than women who work for someone else.

"The worst thing about taking a vacation for an entrepreneur," says Ava Stern, publisher of *Enterprising Women,* "is that the whole time you're away, you're constantly thinking about the office and you're calling the office every day, so what kind of vacation is it? I've had one vacation in ten years."

The toll this may take can be painful. Susan Schein (owner of a public relations firm), who attends the carnival in Trinidad every year to visit friends and break the monotony of a New York winter, didn't go in 1979—and she broke her wrist while skating, which happened, she is sure, because she was too tense and wound up. Vacation is part of her year's plans once again.

If you own your own business, it's difficult to take a long period off, particularly if you're the only one in your office. Frequent three- and four-day weekends are an excellent alternative, as Donna Davis learned. The trick is to take them often; don't let frustrations and tensions build up for months before taking a three-day weekend.

## WALKING AWAY FROM YOUR OWN BUSINESS

Business owners do have the freedom to take an occasional day off in the middle of the week. When I do this, I plan it at least a few days in advance (that's another advantage of the single day off; your plans don't need to be quite as extensive as they would be for two weeks). I complete my priority projects, inform my answering service that I'm off for the day, go home, and lock the door.

A recent Wednesday off found me puttering in the garden, playing with my dog, watching quiz shows (of course), and taking a well-deserved nap. Nothing spectacular, but did I feel good the next day!

Rosemary Gaillard, employee of a family service agency, recognizes our society's belief that "it's OK to take a day off when your physical health is in danger, but it's not OK when your mental health is in danger." Unfortunately, if our mental health is bad enough, the stress will affect physical health.

"I respect employers," continues Gaillard, "who appreciate that good employees need a day sometimes to take care of their mental health. I think if you're a good employee you're not going to abuse it, and I don't. I'm lucky to work for someone who respects that need. I find that I work more effectively after I've taken it."

Since effectiveness is what time management is all about, it's crucial to find some time to get away from your daily workplace surroundings: three weeks or three-day weekends; with a friend or husband or entire family—or by yourself; planned a year in advance or spur of the moment; combined with business or purely for pleasure.

The options are endless. Time for you must include time off.

# *Alone at Last*

---

I want to be alone . . .
—GRETA GARBO

. . .That's why God created Sundays.
—ELLIE HANDSEL
*Owner, art gallery*

NO MATTER how much we love our work, our families and our friends, no matter how much of our time for *us* includes room for others, nearly all of us need time to be absolutely alone.

Single women with no children may sometimes find aloneness a bit too much, but even we know the value of that precious time when there's no one around making demands.

It's time to think, time to zonk out, time to plan, time to play, time to indulge yourself.

The best thing about alone time is that usually a few stolen moments is all it takes, though sometimes an entire day is nice.

## STEALING YOUR OWN MOMENTS

So where do you steal these moments from? By now you should have a pretty good understanding of time management and the importance of time for yourself. You should be able to control your time so those few extra minutes are not an elusive goal, as you may have thought before reading this book. Some ideas:

Get up 15 minutes or an hour earlier than usual to read, plan, have a cup of coffee. Women who do this find the earlier rising hour well worth the relaxation it offers, and for the tone it sets for the rest of the day. And you can be sure of not being interrupted.

Shower time is (usually) alone time. I value this as "thinking" time. Some of my best ideas come to me here. It was also the site of my first "baby steps" to an exercise program.

Drive time is a great time and place. Dr. Doris Moss uses the time to disassociate her workday from the home she is returning to; Jenita Cargile uses it to learn languages; Rosalie Davies practices her singing.

## SOME NEAT ESCAPES

Says training specialist Jackie Friss: "I used to drive an hour to college every morning, and I'd leave the house at six. People would ask how I could do it, but that was my thinking time, and it was the neatest part of the day for me. I could get everything in perspective and change from the home scene and mother to getting into what I really had to do for the day, which was being aware and learning in school. I really feel that sometimes the shower or whatever private time you have helps you to clock yourself and set your schedule for the day."

Bedrooms usually have doors and if you teach your family to respect a closed door (and you don't abuse it), you'll have a private retreat like Rosalie Davies:

"I have my own bedroom and it's on the other side of the house from the other three bedrooms. I also have my own bathroom. This was very important to me when I moved about a year ago. I hide in my bedroom. I have my phone and I have my books and I can be alone here. I leave the door open usually, so they can come in and pester me if they want to, but they're usually off doing their own things."

Many women use the bed itself as a clear signal they want alone time; an entire day in bed with books, television, sewing, or whatever is a great way to be alone:

"Bed is a retreat for me," says Marie McDonald, "and I feel real fine about just staying in bed and reading and watching TV and just cutting back and going into a cocoon. I'm very unsupportive of any effort to break into that cocoon. Every once in a while, on a Saturday or Sunday, or sometimes there have even been entire weekends during times when I've been under a lot of stress. I've done it a lot. When things are going well, maybe once every couple of months. That seems to revitalize and refresh."

Then there's the bath. A number of women say a leisurely soak in the tub is the only alone time they have for themselves.

"Sometimes I just indulge," says Liz Wolff (who plans her life well enough so this is *not* her only alone time), "and am completely decadent and go soak in the tub for about an hour and do a pedicure and just forget about everything."

Take advantage of your "peak" hours, daring to be different. Some people's peak periods provide them with unexpected time alone, if they take advantage of these energy highs and don't fight them.

Ellie Handsel reserves Sundays for sleeping: "I'm very possessive of that time. I think I just come unglued and I spend all day Sunday putting myself back together." Handsel also has a surge of energy between 2:00 and 4:00 a.m. She's alone (very few people have peak periods that coincide with hers) and uses this time to do household chores, read, crochet, do needle-point, exercise. This makes much more sense to her than getting up 15 minutes early, as other women might.

No matter what you do or what signals you send up to acquire this alone time, the need for it is undeniable and its use is a bless-ing: Just forget everything, decompress, relax. People around you must be made aware of this need and the reasons behind it so they can "participate" in your alone time by "getting lost."

Many women get help from their husbands, who'll take the children on an outing to leave mom alone. For some it's a regular event; for others it's as the need arises.

Single women often find themselves alone when their ex-hus-bands take the children for the weekend or summer vacation. If they can't count on this, they should be able to rely on a network, whether it's a formal baby-sitting co-op or a favorite "aunt." Many single, childless women would gladly spend the day in the park with a friend's child.

If all else fails, we can always rely on that old standby—com-munication—to help us: "I say to my daughters," says media director Vicki Riker, " 'I'm going to hear you a lot better when I'm not still all tied up in my head, so give me 30 minutes alone, then let's sit down and talk.' It works."

We began this book because I'd heard so many women say, "I don't have any time for me—I want to have fun!" As our re-search progressed, we found that so many of these women have actually forgotten what fun is.

So now, just for fun, here's a list of things you can do with all the time you've found to manage. It's a compilation of things that the women we know call time for them. You may not find anything you want to do, but it should at least jog your memory and remind you what fun things can be:

## TIME FOR YOU

- reading
- walking
- bicycling
- shopping (leisurely)
- traveling
- morning coffee/newspaper
- entertaining friends
- being entertained
- TV
- movies
- puttering around the house
- just sitting
- gardening
- changing the world
- needlework
- roller skating
- disco dancing
- yoga
- sleeping
- hot bubble baths
- a day in bed
- jogging
- jumping rope
- theater
- the beach
- the mountains
- gourmet cooking
- facials, manicures, pedicures
- painting
- flying lessons
- eating out

Have fun!

# Recommended Reading

*Barter Book, The* by Dyanne Asimow Simon (E. P. Dutton)

*Beyond Sugar and Spice* by Caryl Rivers, Rosalind Barnett, and Grace Baruch (G. P. Putnam's Sons)

*Checklist for a Working Wife* by Marilyn Cooley (Doubleday/Dolphin)

*Creative Woman's Getting-It-All-Together-at-Home Handbook, The* by Jean Ray Laury (Van Nostrand Reinhold)

*Games Mother Never Taught You (Corporate Gamesmanship for Women)* by Betty Lehan Harragan (Rawson Associates Publishers)

*Getting Organized: The Easy Way to Put Your Life in Order* by Stephanie Winston (W. W. Norton)

*Getting Things Done: The ABC's of Time Management* by Edwin C. Bliss (Charles Scribner's Sons)

*Help: A Handbook for Working Mothers* by Barbara Kaye Greenleaf with Lewis A. Schaffer, M.D. (Thomas Y. Crowell)

*How to Get Control of Your Time and Your Life* by Alan Lakein (Peter H. Wyden)

*Management: Tasks-Responsibilities-Practices* by Peter F. Drucker (Harper & Row)

## Recommended Reading

*Managerial Woman, The* by Margaret Hennig and Anne Jardim (Doubleday/Anchor)

*Managing Stress: A Businessperson's Guide* by Jere E. Yates (American Management)

*Mary Ellen's Best of Helpful Hints* by Mary Ellen Pinkham and Pearl Higginbotham (Warner/B. Lansky Books)

*P.E.T.—Parent Effectiveness Training* by Dr. Thomas Gordon (Peter H. Wyden)

*Shower Power* by Helen Fleder (M. Evans)

*Superwoman: For Every Woman Who Hates Housework* by Shirley Conran (Crown Publishers)

*Time Trap, The* by R. Alec Mackenzie (McGraw-Hill)

*Two-Paycheck Family, The* by Caroline Bird (Rawson, Wade Publishers)

*What Color Is Your Parachute? A Practical Manual for Job-Hunters and Career-Changers* by Richard Nelson Bolles (Ten Speed Press)

*Wishcraft: How to Get What You Really Want* by Barbara Sher with Annie Gottlieb (Viking Press)

*Woman's Guide to Management Success, The* by Joan K. Cannie (Prentice-Hall/Spectrum)

*Working Mother's Complete Handbook, The* by Gloria Norris and JoAnn Miller (E. P. Dutton/Sunrise)

*Working Smart: How to Accomplish More In Half the Time* by Michael LeBoeuf (McGraw-Hill)